THE NEW YORK STAGE

FAMOUS PRODUCTIONS IN PHOTOGRAPHS

148 PHOTOS, 1883-1939,
FROM THE THEATRE AND MUSIC COLLECTION
OF THE MUSEUM OF THE CITY OF NEW YORK

EDITED BY STANLEY APPELBAUM

DOVER PUBLICATIONS, INC., NEW YORK

Published in Canada by General Publishing
Company, Ltd., 30 Lesmill Road, Don Mills,
Toronto, Ontario.
Published in the United Kingdom by Constable
and Company, Ltd., 10 Orange Street,
London WC 2.

*The New York Stage: Famous Productions in
Photographs* is a new work, first published by
Dover Publications, Inc., in 1976.

International Standard Book Number: 0-486-23241-7
Library of Congress Catalog Card Number: 75-14558

Manufactured in the United States of America
Dover Publications, Inc., 180 Varick Street,
New York, N.Y. 10014

ACKNOWLEDGMENTS

This project has been from first to last a joint endeavor
of the Museum of the City of New York and Dover
Publications, in which it was my privilege to represent
the publisher and to act as editor.

Unstinting cooperation was offered by all Museum
personnel, special thanks being due to Mr. Joseph
Veach Noble, Director; Mr. A. K. Baragwanath, Senior
Curator; Mrs. Susan McTigue, Registrar; and, of course,
the staff of the Theatre and Music Collection, particularly Mr. Theodore Fetter, Curator; Mr. Grenville Cuy-
ler, Assistant Curator; and Mr. William Richards. The
Theatre and Music Collection staff generously granted
me unusual facilities and access to special categories
of material, thus immeasurably enriching the picture
selection.

I am also deeply grateful to the entire staff of the
Theatre Division of the Library & Museum of the Performing Arts at Lincoln Center, New York, where much
of the research was done, for their infinite patience
and good will in unearthing the materials I needed.

S. A.

INTRODUCTION

From the days of the Greek vase painters and muralists to the present, theatrical scenes have always fascinated artists and those who collect their works. During much of this history, stage performances were recorded in paintings, drawings and prints as souvenirs of enjoyable moments or as proof of the wealth and position of the mighty patrons who paid for the spectacle. With the enormous expansion of commercial advertising in the nineteenth century, publicity became perhaps the chief raison d'être of such depictions. Not only posters and ads, but also artists' renderings of scenes printed in newspapers and magazines, were used to attract audiences.

As photography developed in the first half of the century, it too was pressed into the service of theatrical publicity, but photos appeared chiefly in the form of studio portraits of actors printed on cards, or served merely as the basis for artists' drawings in publications. It was not until quite late in the century that photos could be successfully reproduced economically enough for periodical (and most book) publication, and it was not until 1883 that electrical technology had advanced sufficiently to permit the photographing of a complete scene on stage. This was first done in New York, at the Madison Square Theatre; the play was *A Russian Honeymoon.*

Copies of the historic first scene photo (No. 1 in the present volume) bear the legend: "Photographed in the theatre at midnight, May 1st, 1883, by Falk, 949 Broadway—stage being illuminated by Brush electric lights, put up by Wm. J. Magrath." The photo was autographed by the performers and management. In his book of reminiscences, *Daniel Frohman Presents* (published by Claude Kendall & Willoughby Sharp, N.Y., 1935), Frohman, business manager of the Madison Square Theatre in the early 1880s, provides additional background (p. 57): "A crescent of electric lights was strung across the interior of the theatre to illuminate the stage sufficiently. It took three hours to get everything ready." At nearly the last moment, Frohman decided to get into the picture and donned the uniform of the super who stood at the optical center of the group.

The very next attraction at the Madison Square, *The Rajah,* opening June 5 and intended only as light summer fare, caught on unexpectedly with the public. Its hundredth performance was celebrated by the preparation of a souvenir program containing eight scene photos. Three of these are reproduced here (Nos. 2–4),* showing all the sets. The booklet carries the notice: "The plates forming this Souvenir are reproductions, by the Heliotype Printing Co., Boston, of photographs taken in the Theatre by electric light by Falk, 949 Broadway, N.Y."

It is to these photos from *A Russian Honeymoon* and *The Rajah,* and to their numerous and illustrious New York descendants, that this book is devoted. As often as possible, the photos included here show an entire setting (always with costumed actors in their places on stage), sometimes viewed head on, sometimes from an arresting side angle. Sometimes only a significant portion of the stage is shown, with more emphasis on the performers, but shots that are merely portraits-on-stage, and do not really show the scenic background, have been excluded.

As stage photography became routine, this type of wide-range photo was generally taken at the dress rehearsal. In his knowledgeable and reliable book *Play Production in America* (Henry Holt and Company, N.Y., 1916, p. 311), Arthur Edwin Krows elucidates the conditions in his day:

Dispatch is necessary, mainly because the stage hands, waiting for the photographer to complete his work before "striking" the scene, are being paid for all time on duty, whether active or not.

At conclusion of each act, the photographer, with a couple of assistants, erects his heavy tripod in the auditorium at about the middle of the eighth or tenth row of the orchestra, so as to give his camera proper range for comprehension of the entire stage. Then, in swift succession, by instructions from the producer or stage director, the actors arrange themselves in poses from the preceding action.

Krows points out the usefulness of scene photos for duplicating the settings in stock or road productions. He states that usually from twenty to thirty flashlight pictures were taken per play, but he mentions one production for which only ten were made, and another with over three hundred.

* These reproductions of gravure impressions from the souvenir program are the only items in this volume not reproduced from glossy photographs. All the picture material was kindly lent by the Museum of the City of New York.

Most of the photos in the present volume have been published at one time or another, but chiefly in periodicals contemporary with the productions, and even then rarely in a format sufficiently large to show all the significant details. Those that are also included in books now in print are generally severely cropped there, or else appear all too often in postage-stamp size.

This book is in no way intended as a systematic survey of the New York stage or stagecraft—no one category of play, no one person's career, is represented completely—and yet a broad cross section of both popular and critical successes will be found here. The visual interest of the photos was the uppermost criterion in the selection, but all the productions are important in some way: for their fame and living memory, for quality of script or performance or setting, for their long run, their prizes and awards, inclusion of the play in standard drama courses or anthologies, citation of the scene design in major books on the subject, and so on. "How did that famous or notorious play look?" was the paramount question. Very few revivals, and then only truly noteworthy ones, are represented. In general, these photos show the first New York productions— most frequently, the first productions anywhere.

Although the active foreign-language stage of the city could not be represented, there are distinguished adaptations of plays from the French, German, Italian, Spanish, Russian, Hungarian, Czech and Yiddish. Although no first-rate photos turned up from the Federal Theatre Project, still its most brilliant offspring, the Mercury Theatre, is here, and there are other socially conscious plays of the Thirties. Although stress is placed on the decor and not on the performers, who sometimes appear only as carefully positioned costumed figures, and no special attempt has been made to show the stars of the productions, some of the most eminent actors and actresses of the century are present, as a glance at the Index of Performers will show. The Indexes of Playwrights, Producers, Directors, Set Designers and Costume Designers are also roll calls of top names in the industry. (These indexes make it possible to follow the career of certain personalities—for instance, Jo Mielziner or Richard Bennett—over many years. It is also hoped that such all-but-forgotten names as Ernest Gros, responsible for so many fine sets, may be accorded the recognition they deserve.)

It would be superfluous to point out the wealth of data these pictures contain on dress; home furnishings; trends in stage settings from a dense clutter of properties, through expressionist and constructivist experiments, to a more chaste realism; advances in lighting, and the like. But a close study of these remarkable photos can also reveal more subtle patterns. To take merely one instance, look at the Eugene O'Neill scenes and the George S. Kaufman scenes, and compare the former's intense small groups of people with the latter's crowded stages and flurry of activity. An essential element of their dramaturgy is evident to the eye.

The captions to the pictures give the following information (where available or applicable) in the following order and manner:

The name of the play and the playwright(s); for musicals, the authors of lyrics and music, as well; for translations, the name of the translator(s) or adapter(s); the source in fiction or earlier drama, where applicable. The original foreign-language title (when different) of translated plays is given either at this point or later in the caption. The order of co-authors' names follows the original programs.

The date of the New York opening night of the specific production illustrated. These dates are the basis for the chronological arrangement of the pictures in the book. (The years are repeated in small type just below the pictures. The Alphabetical List of Plays at the beginning of the Indexes is the means for locating titles.) Great care has been taken in every instance to insure that the photo was indeed from the production indicated and not from a later run, but it was very difficult to be sure in a handful of cases.

The New York theater at which the production opened (transfers to other theaters during the course of the original run are usually not given, for reasons of space). The specific photo may not *always* have been taken in this first theater. There is an Index of Theaters, too, at the end of the book; in it, name changes are mentioned only when a theater appears in this book under more than one name.

The number of performances (abbreviated as "perf."), or the closing date, of the original run. When a run resumed after a summer recess, the autumn performances are counted in.

The producer(s), abbreviated as "Prod."

The director(s), abbreviated as "Dir." Over the years, this functionary appears in programs as "stage manager," "stage director," and so on, most often with the credit "staged by." The title here has been regularized, and an attempt has been made to assign the credit correctly. Where this credit or others do not agree with statistics in standard theater chronicles, it is because the original programs or some other published sources have been followed. For musicals, the dance director (choreographer) is also given.

The set designer(s). Where different acts of a single play were designed by various hands (a frequent practice in the nineteenth and early twentieth centuries), it is made clear who designed the particular set illustrated. Set builders or painters are credited here only when there was no other set credit in the original programs. For reasons of space, designers or providers of set accessories or dressings have been omitted.

The costume designer(s). Most of these credits were available only on the original programs. Here again, only the designers, and not the executants, are given, unless there was no other credit. Designers of specific dresses or specific actors' and actresses' wardrobes are given only when their handiwork is visible in the photos.

Special credits for lighting and mechanical effects are given in the few available instances.

The information that occurs next in the captions is possibly the most significant, and certainly of a type exceedingly rare in theatrical publications: an attempt has been made to identify not only the particular act and scene (giving the locale in sufficient detail) of each photo, but also the specific moment of the action that is depicted. In outlining this action, we give the names of the characters that are shown, followed, *in parentheses*, by the names of the actors performing the roles. Once in a while, the identifications of performers are based on original-cast listings or other similar indications rather than on personal recognition, but every care has been taken in our research to insure reasonable accuracy. Only rarely is an actor mentioned who is not depicted. It should be noted that in describing the scenes and the position of the actors, "left" and "right" always mean the left and right of the printed picture, and *not* "stage left" or "stage right."

The next part of most of the captions contains a miscellany of facts that will hopefully be of interest. For revivals, as well as first New York productions of British plays or plays from California (etc.), and translations from Continental plays, the date and place of the world premiere are given as fully as possible. (Where there is no indication to the contrary, the production pictured is the premiere—never counting out-of-town tryouts.) Other data in this section may pertain to the careers of individuals connected with the play, the mechanics of the setting, length of run, real-life sources of the plot, and so on. Pulitzer Prizes and New York Drama Critics Circle Awards are always mentioned. Rigidly excluded from the book is one category of information that would have become a tail wagging the dog: no reference whatsoever is made to film versions of the plays.

The last element in each caption, where known—always given in parentheses—is the photographer or photographic studio responsible for the picture. For biographical data on performers, playwrights, designers, directors, and the like, the reader should consult the standard theatrical references and books by or about the personalities.

Information on the photographers, however, is relatively harder to come by, and since it is their work that this book is "all about," the following information is offered. (To relate the names to the photos, see the Index of Photographers at the end of the volume.)

Pride of place goes to the creator of on-stage scene photography, Benjamin Joseph Falk, born in New York City on October 14, 1853. At the time of *A Russian Honeymoon,* his studio was located on what was to be the site of the Flatiron Building; later he moved his business to the Waldorf-Astoria. Falk's work included other types of art and commercial photography as well. He died on March 19, 1925.

The photo credit "Byron" refers to an entire family, headed in the era represented here by Joseph Byron, born in Nottingham, England, in 1844, the year in which the family's photo business was founded. Joseph Byron came to New York in 1888. His stage photography began in 1891. This line, and the photographing of ship interiors (chiefly handled by Joseph's son Percy), comprised the firm's main business, but on various assignments the Byrons snapped almost every conceivable type of exterior and interior in the city. Joseph Byron died in 1923. The firm, which then included the fifth generation of photographic Byrons, closed down in 1942, but Percy Byron continued to work for others.

The credit "Hall" stands for George P. Hall & Son, located at 212 Broadway. Like the Byrons, the Halls in their career combined stage scenes with street scenes; for instance, they took photos of turn-of-the-century subway construction.

The credit "White" refers to the firm of L. S. White, or the White Studio. Luther S. White, located at 1546 Broadway, was responsible, along with his associate Lucas (on whom more below), for the development of the flash pan and the flare type of photography for theater work.

Florence Vandamm, born in London, died at the age of 83 on March 15, 1966. In 1918, still in England, she married another photographer, George R. Thomas, a native of Washington, D.C. According to the *New York Times* obituary of Mrs. Thomas, the couple came to the U.S. in 1923, but there are clear Vandamm stamps on photos reproduced here that are indubitably of 1920 and 1922 New York productions. At any rate, the Thomases, i.e., the Vandamm organization, covered some 2000 shows from the early Twenties on. Mr. Thomas, known professionally as Tommy Vandamm, did most of the stage photography until his death in 1944. Until then, Florence Vandamm was mainly concerned with taking the portraits of the performers in costume in her 130 West 57th Street studio. After 1944, she handled both ends of the work until her retirement in 1950.

George W. Lucas, another specialist in stage photography, was born in Toronto on November 4, 1877. He came to New York in 1905. About ten years later he became associated with Luther S. White (see above), and remained with the White Studios until 1936. He then opened his own studio at 17 East 48th Street, at first in association with Irving Pritchard (Lucas-Pritchard, Inc.), then, in 1939, with Edward Thayer Monroe (Lucas & Monroe, Inc). Before 1939, Monroe had been located at 18 East 46th Street. Lucas retired in 1941, and died on May 28, 1942.

Francis Bruguière, who had a studio at 10 West 49th Street, worked for the Theatre Guild in its early years. He is also represented here by a Neighborhood Playhouse photo. He died at his London home in May of 1945.

Paul Thompson, a pioneer independent news photographer, was not an expert cameraman himself, but had a stable of skilled anonymous employees. He covered all kinds of events, and did not specialize in stage work. He began his career as a (writing) journalist, switching permanently to photography after doing a very lucrative series of pictures of Mark Twain at home.

James Abbe, born in 1882, took important news (and other) photos from 1898 (a shot of the battleship *Maine* while it was still intact) through World War II. In 1917 he set up a studio in the Hotel des Artistes in New York. In 1924 he left for Europe. After the Second World War he worked in radio and TV on the West Coast until 1961. He died in San Francisco on November 12, 1973, at the age of 91.

Alfred Cheney Johnston, an "arty" photographer specializing in portraits, high-class nudes in sylvan glades, and so on, was quite appropriately associated with Florenz Ziegfeld's shows for a number of years beginning in 1918. His 1919 photo of *The Jest* has truly rich tones.

When Drix Duryea took the *Garrick Gaieties* photo in 1926, his studio was at 126 East 59th Street.

This book is a tribute to these scene photographers.

1883

1

A RUSSIAN HONEYMOON, by Mrs. Burton N. (Constance Cary) Harrison (adapted from *La lune de miel* by Eugène Scribe, Mélesville [A. H. J. Duveyrier] & P. F. A. Carmouche). April 9, 1883. Madison Square Theatre. Ran through June 2, 1883. Prod.: Daniel Frohman. Dir.: Franklin H. Sargent & David Belasco. Sets: Mazzanovich & W. H. Lippincott. Act 2, the home of the master shoemaker Ivan Gavrilovitch in Russian Poland, 1850. This is the closing tableau of the act; to judge by the French original, it was at this moment that the Hungarian noblewoman Poleska (Agnes Booth, beside the spinning wheel) had her husband Alexis Petrovitch (Frederic Bryton, near center, being held back by rifles) arrested by the local authorities. He had first told her he was Gustave Count Woroffski, then informed her he was merely a serf and a cobbler (he really was the Count, and undertook the pretense to cure her of her pride). The tall, slim man in the very center is not one of the actors, but the producer, Daniel Frohman. The play was first performed at special matinees on Dec. 28 & 29, 1882, by a group of society amateurs including Mrs. James Brown Potter. This was the first on-stage scene photograph. Further details in Introduction. (Photo: Falk)

1883

2
THE RAJAH, or WYNCOT'S WARD, by William Young. June 5, 1883. Madison Square Theatre. Ran through Jan. 29, 1884. Prod.: Daniel Frohman. Dir.: Franklin H. Sargent & David Belasco. Sets: Mazzanovich & W. H. Lippincott, and Dayton. Act 1, the exterior of Wyncot Lodge, England (set by Mazzanovich & Lippincott). The indolent and amatory Harold Wyncot (H. M. Pitt), whom his fellow cavalry officers in India nicknamed "The Rajah," arrives at the home of his late uncle, who made him his heir and the guardian of Gladys, an adopted daughter. Servants, estate managers and neighbors are on hand to greet him. At the left is Buttons, the housekeeper's son (Alfred Klein). Further details in Introduction. (Photo: Falk)

1883

3

THE RAJAH. Act 3, a glade in the park of Wyncot Lodge (set by Mazzanovich & Lippincott). Gladys (Carrie Turner) and her friend Emilia Jekyll (Marion Elmore) are vexed to find that Buttons has preceded them even to this remote nook (he has been assigned by Harold to follow them everywhere, since there is danger from disgruntled workmen, and the girls find this supervision tyrannical). Real running water was a feature of this scene. Alfred Klein, seen here as Buttons, was a brother of Charles Klein, author of *The Lion and the Mouse,* and of Manuel Klein, who composed the scores of the earliest Hippodrome shows. (Photo: Falk)

1883

4
THE RAJAH. Act 4 (same set as Act 2), The drawing room of Wyncot Lodge (set by Dayton). The chief labor agitator, Cragin (Max Freeman), actually an escaped convict, has broken into the house, but is held at bay by the really dauntless Harold, who has Gladys by his side. (Photo: Falk)

1890

5

BLUE JEANS, by Joseph Arthur. Oct. 6, 1890. Fourteenth Street Theatre. First run ended Mar. 7, 1891. Dir.: Ben Teal. Sets: Homer F. Emens. Mechanical effects by J. E. De Beauvais & Son and Edward Peck. Act 3, Scene 3, interior of Perry Bascom's sawmill on the banks of the Ohio River in Indiana. Bascom (Robert Hilliard) has been knocked out and designated as mincemeat by his mill foreman Ben Boone (George Fawcett), who is in love with Bascom's cruel and resentful first wife (divorced by Bascom because of her bigamy). June, the new Mrs. Bascom (Jennie Yeamans), has been locked in the mill office, but she breaks out. This often-imitated scene marks one of the high points of nineteenth-century melodrama of suspense and stage effects. The play was also noted for its sentiment over a daughter gone to the city and gone bad; this inspired the 1891 song "The Picture That Is Turned Toward the Wall." There was also much light entertainment, with a band, singers and real doves and cows. The actors listed above are those of the opening-night cast; it is not certain that they are the ones in the photo.

6
THE LITTLE MINISTER, by James M. Barrie. Sept. 27, 1897. Empire Theatre. 300 perf. Prod.: Charles Frohman. Dir.: Joseph Humphreys. Sets & costumes: Edward G. Unitt. Act 2, Scene 1, Nanny Webster's cottage. The young minister Gavin Dishart (Robert Edeson) visits Nanny Webster (Kate Ten Eyck) and finds that the strange girl Babbie (Maude Adams) has returned Nanny's cloak and bonnet with which she had disguised herself at their last meeting. This was Maude Adams' first starring part, and the beginning of her long association with Barrie roles. The play did not open in London until Nov. 6, 1897 (at the Haymarket). (Photo: Byron)

1898

7
WAY DOWN EAST, by Lottie Blair Parker (elaborated by Joseph R. Grismer). Feb. 7, 1898. Manhattan Theatre. 152 perf. Prod.: William A. Brady & Florenz Ziegfeld (Jr.). Sets: Hugh Logan Reid, St. John Lewis & John H. Young. Act 3 (set by St. John Lewis), a combination living and dining room in the Bartlett farmhouse in New England. Climax of act: Anna Moore, homeless girl taken on as a servant by the Bartletts, who now wish to cast her out because she has had an illegitimate child, names wealthy scheming neighbor Lennox Sanderson as the villain who deceived her by a mock marriage. Left to right: Louisa Bartlett (Sara Stevens); Squire Amasa Bartlett (Odell Williams); their step-niece Kate Brewster (Minnie Dupree); neighbor Martha Perkins (Ella Hugh Wood); visiting entomologist Professor Sterling (George Backus); Anna (Phoebe Davies); David, the Bartlett son who loves her (Howard Kyle); Sanderson (Frank Lander). One of the great theatrical moneymakers, playing on the road for many years, *Way* (or *'Way*) *Down East* was first performed in Newport, R.I., on Aug. 28, 1897; the first performance of the doctored, or "elaborated," version (the elaboration included the mechanical snowstorm in the last act) took place in Chicago on Nov. 19, 1897. (Photo: Byron)

1898

8
THE LIARS, by Henry Arthur Jones. Sept. 26, 1898. Empire Theatre. 112 perf. Prod.: Charles Frohman. Dir.: Joseph Humphreys. Sets: Edward G. Unitt. Act 1, the interior of a large tent on the lawn of a wealthy home in the Thames valley. As the visiting celebrity Edward Falkner (Arthur Byron) reads the Colonial Office note requesting him to return to Africa, his sagacious friend Colonel Sir Christopher Deering (John Drew) awaits his decision as do (left) Beatrice Ebernoe (Blanche Burton) and Lady Jessica Nepean (Isabelle Irving). Usually considered the finest effort of Jones, a master of high comedy of manners, *The Liars* was originally produced at the Criterion Theatre, London, on Oct. 6, 1897. John Drew was, of course, the maternal uncle of Ethel, Lionel and John Barrymore. (Photo: Byron)

1898

9
CYRANO DE BERGERAC, by Edmond Rostand (translated by Howard Thayer Kingsbury). Oct. 3, 1898. Garden Theatre. 48 perf. Prod. & dir.: Richard Mansfield. Sets: Richard Marston. Act 1, the theater in the Hôtel de Bourgogne, Paris, in 1640. Cyrano (Richard Mansfield), who has a grudge against the star, interrupts the performance and indulges in swordplay. The world premiere of *Cyrano* took place at the Théâtre de la Porte-Saint-Martin, Paris, on Dec. 28, 1897. Mansfield's production was the first authorized one in America, although several pirated versions competed with his. One of these was produced by Augustin Daly in Philadelphia on the same night that Mansfield's opened in New York, but Daly's was a quick failure.

1898

10

THE CHRISTIAN, by Hall Caine (from his own novel). Oct. 10, 1898. Knickerbocker Theatre. 160 perf. Prod.: Liebler & Co. Dir.: Hall Caine (mob scenes by Frank Keenan). Sets: Louis C. Young. Act 2, the clubroom of St. Mary Magdalene's, Soho. Act finale: the idealistic young clergyman John Storm (Edward J. Morgan, far left), aided by Brother Paul (Frank Keenan), restrains the angry crowd of parishioners to whom he has just revealed that the greedy and godless owners of the property want to demolish the church in order to enlarge their music hall. A popular romantic success of its day, *The Christian* had a copyright performance (a legal technicality) in England in 1897, but its formal London opening did not occur until Oct. 16, 1899 (Duke of York's Theatre). (Photo: Byron)

1899

11
ZAZA, by Pierre Berton & Charles Simon (adapted from the French by David Belasco). Jan. 9, 1899. Garrick Theatre. 184 perf. Prod.: Charles Frohman. Dir.: David Belasco. Sets: Ernest Gros. Act 5, outside the Concert des Ambassadeurs on the Champs-Elysées. Preceded by her maid Nathalie (Maria Davis), the music-hall singer Zaza (Mrs. Leslie Carter), now the toast of Paris, leaves the theater after her perform-ance, while her former lover Bernard Dufrene (Charles A. Stevenson) waits to ask her to return to him. *Zaza,* one of the triumphs of Belasco star Mrs. Leslie Carter, a society divorcée, was first produced in its original French at the Théâtre du Vaudeville, Paris, on May 12, 1898. In Paris its great popularity was due largely to the brilliant perform-ance of the actress Réjane. (Photo: Byron)

1899

12
CHILDREN OF THE GHETTO, by Israel Zangwill (from his own book of sketches). Oct. 16, 1899. Herald Square Theatre. 49 perf. Prod.: Liebler & Co. Dir.: James A. Herne. Sets: Frank E. Gates & E. A. Morange. Act 4, a marketplace in the Jewish district of London's East End on the eve of Passover, about 1875. During this final act the orthodox rabbi's daughter is nearly persuaded by the man she loves to run off with him to America, since a bizarre technicality of Jewish law prevents their marriage at home. New York enjoyed the first view of this unusual slice-of-life play, which was not mounted in London until Dec. 11, 1899 (Adelphi Theatre), and then with an American company. The director, Herne, was the author of the immensely popular play *Shore Acres*. (Photo: Byron)

Byron n.Y.
8033

1899

13
SHERLOCK HOLMES, by William Gillette (with the cooperation of Arthur Conan Doyle). Nov. 6, 1899. Garrick Theatre.
256 perf. Prod.: Charles Frohman. Dir.: William Postance.
Sets: Ernest Gros. Act 2, Scene 2, the drawing room of
Holmes's apartment on Baker Street. Billy the pageboy
(Henry McArdle) waits at the door as the Napoleon of crime,
Professor Moriarty (George Wessells), leaves in a rage—
he has failed either to scare off or to murder the imper-
turbable Holmes (William Gillette). Actually, at this point
of the play, Billy's coat should be off and his shirt and
vest torn. This drama has had an enviable history of revivals
up to 1974. Gillette himself played the title role in New
York as late as 1929, touring until 1931. (Photo: Byron)

1901

14

THE CLIMBERS, by Clyde Fitch. Jan. 21, 1901. Bijou Theatre. 163 perf. Prod.: Amelia Bingham. Dir.: Clyde Fitch. Sets: Joseph A. Physioc & Ernest Albert. Amelia Bingham's gowns by Robert Osborn, Annie Irish's by J. Blaine & Co. Act 2 (set by Physioc), the dining room of the Hunter mansion on Christmas Eve. Ned Warden accuses his old friend Dick Sterling, a stock-market speculator, of embezzling the funds of Sterling's wife's aunt that had been entrusted to Sterling. Left to right: the aunt, Ruth Hunter (Annie Irish); Sterling (Frank Worthing); Warden (Robert Edeson); Blanche Hunter Sterling, Dick's wife (Amelia Bingham); and family friend Frederick Mason (John Flood). Immediately after this moment, the lights in the "room" were turned out, and Sterling made his confession in the dark—an imaginative bit of theater, but unsuitable for photography! Note the stained glass, pillars and other features of wealthy homes of the period, so well observed by Clyde Fitch; Chauncey Depew's home in New York was adorned with painted friezes like the one in this set. (Photo: Byron)

1901

15
CAPTAIN JINKS OF THE HORSE MARINES, by Clyde Fitch. Feb. 4, 1901. Garrick Theatre. 192 perf. Prod.: Charles Frohman. Dir.: Joseph Humphreys (supervised by Clyde Fitch). Sets: Edward G. Unitt. Costumes: Percy Anderson & from *Godey's Lady's Book* for 1872. Act 2, the opera singer Madame Trentoni's hotel room in the Brevoort House, New York, early 1870s. Madame Trentoni, actually an American, Aurelia Johnson (Ethel Barrymore), leans on the arm of her teacher, Professor Belliarti (Edwin Stevens), as she informs her companion, Mrs. Greenborough (Estelle Mortimer), that she has just accepted the marriage proposal of the romantic young Captain Jinks. Ethel Barrymore became a star during the run of this lightweight comedy, the success of which was due chiefly to her performance. (Photo: Byron)

1901

16

UNDER TWO FLAGS, by Paul M. Potter (from the novel by Ouida). Feb. 5, 1901. Garden Theatre. 135 perf. Prod.: Charles Frohman (by arrangement with David Belasco). Dir.: Max Freeman (Belasco gave advice and coached Blanche Bates). Sets: Ernest Gros. Costumes: Dazian. Act 4, Scene 2, Chellala Gorge in Algeria. The impetuous vivandière Cigarette (Blanche Bates, wearing boots), bearing a stay of execution that will save the Legionnaire she loves, is delayed by Arabs. This celebrated mountain set was made of closely dove-tailing sections that moved on casters. It concealed a zigzag ramp (where the Arabs are standing). At the end of the scene, Cigarette, in danger from the Arabs, flees on her pony under cover of a sandstorm (created solely by light and sound effects) and rides up the ramp and off stage, thus out-Mazeppa-ing Adah Isaacs Menken. The endlessly influential 1867 novel had been dramatized at least four times previously in England and America, but this was the most elaborate version.

1901

17

IF I WERE KING, by Justin Huntly McCarthy (from his own story). Oct. 14, 1901. Garden Theatre. 56 perf. Prod.: Daniel Frohman. Dir.: William Seymour. Sets: Edward G. Unitt. Costumes: Ogden. Act 4, an open place in Paris in the fifteenth century. François Villon (E. H. Sothern), condemned to be hanged even though he is still fresh from his victory over the Burgundians, is saved when the haughty noblewoman Katherine de Vaucelles (Cecilia Loftus—for a while the author's wife) promises to marry him. On the dais: King Louis XI (George W. Wilson), with the Queen (Margaret B. Caskie). The Anglo-Irishman McCarthy's romantic perennial, which was to be closely followed in the text of Friml's operetta *The Vagabond King,* was not produced in London until Aug. 30, 1902 (at the St. James's Theatre).

1902

18

THE STUBBORNNESS OF GERALDINE, by Clyde Fitch. Nov. 3, 1902. Garrick Theatre. 64 perf. Prod.: Frank McKee. Dir.: Clyde Fitch. Sets: Joseph A. Physioc. Mary Mannering's gowns by Paquin of Paris & Mme Simcox of New York. Act 1, the deck of an ocean liner. Geraldine Lang (Mary Mannering), a New York girl returning from Europe after many years, is wooed by an impoverished Hungarian, Count Carlos Kinsey (Arthur Byron), who sings her an old Viennese love song, accompanying himself pizzicato on the violin. Fitch's thorough acquaintance with the haunts of the wealthy included not only their homes, but such entertaining and novel locales (for the stage of his day) as the deck of a luxury liner. (Photo: Byron)

1902

19
THE STICKINESS OF GELATINE, by Edgar Smith; lyrics by Edgar Smith & Robert B. Smith; music by W. T. Francis & John Stromberg. Late Dec. 1902. Weber & Fields' Music Hall. Prod.: Weber & Fields. Dir.: Julian Mitchell. Sets: P. J. McDonald. Costumes & gowns: Will R. Barnes. In this giddy spoof of *The Stubbornness of Geraldine,* the characters were, from left to right: Lord Spillberries (Peter F. Dailey); Vi Bumpson of Tombstone, Arizona (William Collier); Fräulein Krank, Gelatine's companion (Joseph M. Weber); Gelatine Pang (Fay Templeton); Count Careless Kidney (Lew M. Fields); Mrs. Brightun (Louise Allen, wife of William Collier); Mr. Brightun (Charles A. Bigelow); unidentified. *The Stickiness of Gelatine* was just one of several successive second parts of the bill offered in the Weber & Fields show *Twirly Whirly* (opened Sept. 11, 1902; 244 perf.). Each of these second halves parodied a new Broadway play. The producers of the "victimized" plays enjoyed the fun and the publicity, and gave Weber & Fields's staff special early viewing privileges. (Photo: Byron)

1902

20

THE ETERNAL CITY, by Hall Caine (from his own novel). Nov. 17, 1902. Victoria Theatre. 92 perf. Prod.: Liebler & Co. Act 1, Scene 1, the loggia of Baron Bonelli's palace, overlooking St. Peter's Square, Rome, "in the near future." Donna Roma Volonna (Viola Allen), capricious and spoiled ward of the all-powerful prime minister Bonelli (Frederic de Belleville), promises to win the confidence of the young revolutionary who has publicly insulted her, and then to betray him to the government. Another Hall Caine mélange of religion, revolution and romance, *The Eternal City* had a "simultaneous" production (actually a little earlier, starting October 2) in London at His Majesty's Theatre. (Photo: Byron)

1902

21
THE DARLING OF THE GODS, by David Belasco & John Luther Long. Dec. 3, 1902. Belasco Theatre. 246 perf. Prod. & dir.: David Belasco. Sets: Ernest Gros. Costumes: Genjiro Yeto. Act 1, the banquet room of Prince Saigon of Tosan in Japan, set for "The Feast of a Thousand Welcomes." As the wounded guest of honor, the outlaw Kara (Robert T. Haines), praises the independence of the old samurai warriors, Yo-San, the Prince's daughter (Blanche Bates), disguised as a geisha to gain admittance to the group, recognizes the young man as the one who recently saved her life and her father's. Left of her, with staring eyes, is Prince Saigon (Charles Walcot); immediately below her outstretched hand is the impassive minister of war, Zakkuri (George Arliss); next to the pillar at the right is the geisha Rosy Sky (Eleanor Moretti). The authors had already collaborated on the one-act *Madame Butterfly* in 1900. *The Darling of the Gods* had several stunning visual effects, particularly the final transformation from the River of Souls to the First Celestial Heaven. (Photo: Byron)

1904

22

CANDIDA, by George Bernard Shaw. Jan. 4, 1904. Madison Square Theatre. 133 perf. Prod. & dir.: Arnold Daly. The drawing room of St. Dominic's Parsonage, overlooking Victoria Park, in the northeast quarter of London. Act 2: the Parson's typist, Proserpine Garnett (Louise Closser, later Louise Closser Hale), has an argument with his father-in-law, Mr. Burgess (Herbert Standing), while the young poet Eugene Marchbanks (Arnold Daly) waits despondently. Arnold Daly came into prominence through this first professional production of *Candida* in New York. Before the regular run opened at the Madison Square, there had been special matinees at the Princess beginning Dec. 9, 1903. In Britain, after a copyright performance in 1895, the play was given at Her Majesty's Theatre, Aberdeen, from July 30, 1897, and at the Strand Theatre, London, from July 1, 1900. (Photo: Byron)

1904

23
MRS. WIGGS OF THE CABBAGE PATCH, by Anne Crawford Flexner (from two books by Alice Hegan Rice, *Mrs. Wiggs of the Cabbage Patch & Lovey Mary).* Sept. 3, 1904. Savoy Theatre. 150 perf. Prod.: Liebler & Co. Dir.: Oscar Eagle. Act 3, the exterior of Mrs. Wiggs's tin-roof house. Mrs. Wiggs (Madge Carr Cook) persuades Lucy (Nora Shelby) to marry the newspaperman Bob (Thurston Hall) even though it means following him to the North. In the background, romance buds between Mrs. Wiggs's son Billy (Argyle Campbell) and the orphan Lovey Mary whom she is sheltering (Mabel Talia-ferro). A good example of an adroit dramatization of highly popular fiction, *Mrs. Wiggs* was on the road almost a year before reaching New York. Madge Carr Cook was the mother of the actress Eleanor Robson (Mrs. August Belmont, patron of the Metropolitan Opera). (Photo: Byron)

1904

24

LEAH KLESCHNA, by C. M. S. McLellan. Dec. 12, 1904. Manhattan Theatre. 155 perf. Prod. & dir.: Minnie Maddern Fiske & Harrison Grey Fiske. Sets: Frank E. Gates & E. A. Morange. Mrs. Fiske's costumes by Mme E. S. Freisinger. Act 1, the lodgings of the Austrian jewel thief Kleschna, alias Garnier, on the Rue de Clichy, Paris. Left to right: Kleschna's associate Schram (William B. Mack), posing as a servant, and hopelessly in love with Kleschna's daughter Leah; Leah, who does the actual housebreaking (Mrs. Fiske); Kleschna (Charles Cartwright); the dissipated Raoul Berton (George Arliss), who wants Leah to live with him, and who has been giving Kleschna information about the next house to be robbed. The playwright McLellan, under the pseudonym Hugh Morton, had already written the books of several important musicals, especially *The Belle of New York*. This, his first serious effort, was guided to success in the writing and in the directing by Mrs. Fiske. (Photo: Byron)

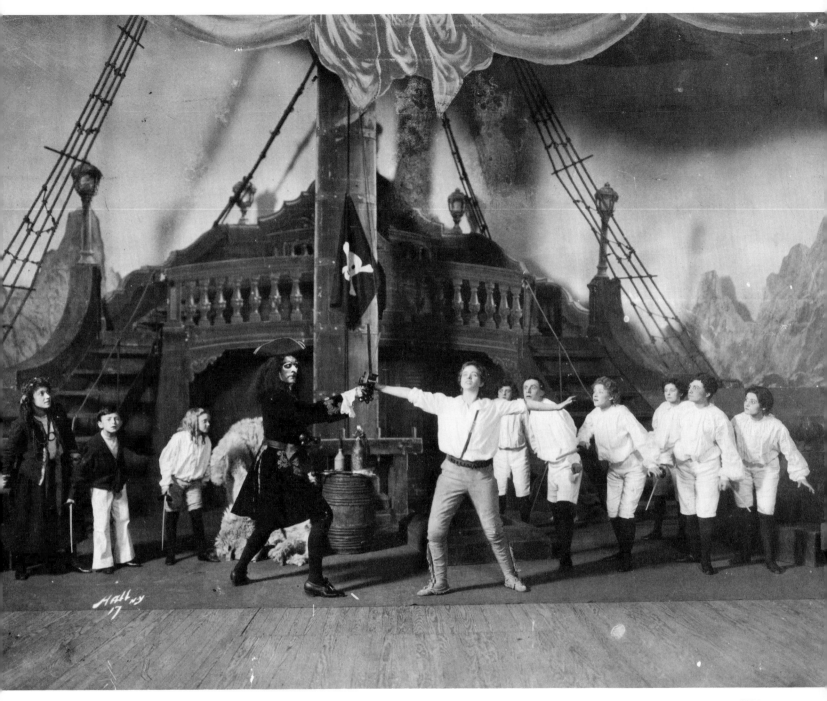

1905

25
PETER PAN, by James M. Barrie. Nov. 6, 1905. Empire Thea-
tre. 263 perf. Prod.: Charles Frohman. Dir.: J. M. Francouer.
Sets: Ernest Gros. Act 5, Scene 1, the pirate ship. Peter
(Maude Adams) arrives to fight Captain Jas. Hook (Ernest
Lawford) and rescue the lost boys (right) and the Darling
children, Wendy (Mildred Morris), John (Walter Robinson)
and Michael (Martha McGraw). This was the first American
production of the frequently revived and adapted classic.
The original production was at the Duke of York's Theatre,
London, on Dec. 27, 1904, with Nina Boucicault, daughter of
the playwright Dion Boucicault, as Peter. (Photo: Hall)

1905

26

THE GIRL OF THE GOLDEN WEST, by David Belasco. Nov. 14, 1905. Belasco Theatre. 224 perf. Prod. & dir.: David Belasco. Sets: Ernest Gros. Costumes: Mme E. S. Freisinger. Act 1, in the Polka Saloon, near Cloudy Mountain, California, 1849. The sheriff, Jack Rance (Frank Keenan, left), is disturbed by the attention paid by the proprietress—Minnie—the Girl (Blanche Bates)—to the new arrival, Dick Johnson, really the bandit Ramerrez (Robert Hilliard). At the beginning of the play, there was an effect of lights and screens like a filmic dissolve, showing first Minnie's cabin on the mountain, then the exterior of the saloon, and finally this interior. Belasco, born in San Francisco not long after the Gold Rush began, here celebrated his home state. (Photo: Byron)

1905

27
THE GIRL OF THE GOLDEN WEST. Act 4, the boundless prairies of the West. The former saloonkeeper and the former outlaw look to the dawn of a new day and a new life. Belasco devoted the same scrupulous care to scenes of the great outdoors. He was also to direct the world premiere of *La Fanciulla del West*, Puccini's opera based on this play, at the Metropolitan Opera House in 1910. (Photo: Byron)

1905

28
THE LION AND THE MOUSE, by Charles Klein. Nov. 20, 1905. Lyceum Theatre. 686 perf. Prod.: Henry B. Harris. Dir.: William Harris & R. A. Roberts. Sets: Joseph A. Physioc. Grace Elliston's gowns by Ward. Act 3, the inner private library in the Ryder mansion on Fifth Avenue. Shirley Rossmore (Grace Elliston), who has entered the home of capitalist John Burkett Ryder (Edmund Breese) under false pretenses in order to gain proof that he unjustly ruined her father's professional reputation, finally reveals her identity to him, while his son Jefferson, whom she loves (Richard Bennett), realizes this will ruin their chance of marriage. This improbable but likable love story, with its main theme of a girl's pluck and independence, enjoyed the longest New York run up to its time. (Photo: White)

1906

29
GEORGE WASHINGTON, JR., by George M. Cohan (book, lyrics & music). Feb. 12, 1906. Herald Square Theatre. 81 perf. Prod.: Sam H. Harris. Dir.: George M. Cohan. Sets: John H. Young & Ernest Albert. Ethel Levey's hats & gowns by Hitchins & Balcom and Lord & Taylor. Act 1, outside Mount Vernon (set by John Young). George Belgrave (George M. Cohan), superpatriotic son of a Senator, sings "The Grand Old Rag" (soon changed to "You're a Grand Old Flag"). This is a cast line-up rather than the actual scene, since not all these characters were on stage for that number. Among the others are: at the left, George's excessively European-oriented father, Senator James Belgrave (Jerry J. Cohan, George M.'s father); to the right of him, Mrs. Stebbins, the Senator's sister (Helen F. Cohan, George M.'s mother); seated at the right, Senator Belgrave's professional rival, Senator William Hopkins (Eugene O'Rourke), and his niece, Dolly Johnson (Ethel Levey, George M.'s wife at the time), who sang "I Was Born in Virginia" in the same act. (Photo: Hall)

"The Rose Of The Rancho"

1906

30

THE ROSE OF THE RANCHO, by David Belasco & Richard Walton Tully. Nov. 27, 1906. Belasco Theatre. 327 perf. Prod. & dir.: David Belasco. Sets: Ernest Gros. Costumes: Albertine Randall Wheelan. Act 2, the patio of the Castro-Kenton rancho, San Juan, California, in the late 1850s. Juanita Castro, the "Rose of the Rancho," is perturbed to see the man she loves, the U.S. government agent Kearney, arrive at her evening betrothal party in the company of the villainous land jumper Kinkaid. Left to right: Juanita's mother, Señora Kenton (Grace Gayler Clark); a servant; Juanita's grandmother, Doña Petrona Castro (Marta Melean); Padre Antonio (Frank Losee); Juanita (Frances Starr); a servant; Juanita's unloved fiancé, Don Luis de la Torre (Hamilton Revelle); Kearney (Charles Richman); and Kinkaid (John W. Cope). This tale of California, set in the years of Belasco's boyhood there, was also related to current events: deplorable evictions of landowners that took place in 1903. (Photo: Byron)

1907

31
THE WITCHING HOUR, by Augustus Thomas. Nov. 18, 1907. Hackett Theatre. 212 perf. Prod.: Sam S. & Lee Shubert, Inc. Act 3, the library and card room at Jack Brookfield's elegant gambling establishment in Louisville. The very end of the act and the climax of the play: the crooked district attorney Frank Hardmuth (George Nash) cannot kill the man who has exposed him, Brookfield (William Morris), because of the latter's hypnotic power, aided by that of psychic Judge Prentice (Russ Whytal). The role of Brookfield was created by John Mason. This popular play made capital out of the current interest in mental telepathy. (Photo: Hall)

1908

32
SALVATION NELL, by Edward Sheldon. Nov. 17, 1908. Hackett Theatre. 71 perf. Prod.: Harrison Grey Fiske. Dir.: Minnie Maddern Fiske & Harrison Grey Fiske. Sets: D. Frank Dodge & Ernest Gros. Costumes: Mme E. S. Freisinger. Act 1 (set by Dodge), the Empire Bar at Tenth Avenue and 48th Street, New York, on Christmas Eve. Nell Sanders (Mrs. Fiske), charwoman of the bar, begs her shiftless and faithless lover Jim Platt (Holbrook Blinn) to stop drinking and talk to her about their future. When the Fiskes accepted the play, Sheldon was still a Harvard senior, studying in George Pierce Baker's famous drama workshop. The mahogany-and-brass bar, and other stage furnishings in Act 1, were authentic pieces acquired at auction. This set and the realistic Act 3 slum street corner gave pause—and even further stimulus—to Belasco.

1909

33

THE EASIEST WAY, by Eugene Walter. Jan. 19, 1909. Stuyvesant Theatre. 157 perf. Prod. & dir.: David Belasco. Sets: Ernest Gros. Gowns by Mollie O'Hara. Act 2, Laura Murdock's furnished room, second story back, in a cheap theatrical lodging house in New York. Annie, the house servant (Marion Kerby), hands a dunning note to Laura (Frances Starr), an actress out of work, who used to be kept by a rich man but is now struggling to live straight so she and a low-paid Western reporter can marry. The chorine Elfie St. Clair (Laura Nelson Hall), still a kept woman, is visiting Laura to urge her to reconsider and return to luxury. This play was noted for its unconventionally unhappy ending and for this set, which achieved photographic realism again by use of real articles of furniture and decor. (Photo: White)

1909

34
ANTONY AND CLEOPATRA, by William Shakespeare. Nov. 6, 1909. New Theatre. Performed in repertory. Sets: Ernest Albert, from drawings by Jules Guerin. Act 4, Scene 15, a monument in Alexandria. Cleopatra (Julia Marlowe) sorrows over the dying Antony (E. H. Sothern); at the left, Iras (Leah Bateman-Hunter), at the right, Charmian (Jessie Busley), Cleopatra's attendants. This unsuccessful production, the first offering of the New Theatre, boded ill for the future of this "national" art repertory house endowed by New York millionaires. The New Theatre scheme lasted only until May 1911; the house was later reopened as the highly commercial Century Theatre. *Antony and Cleopatra* was probably first performed at Blackfriars, London, in 1608. (Photo: Garraway-Byron)

35
THE BLUE BIRD, by Maurice Maeterlinck (translated by Alexander Teixeira de Mattos). Oct. 1, 1910. New Theatre. 145 perf. Dir.: George Foster Platt. Sets: Edward G. Unitt & Wickes. Costumes: Mrs. L. Peck. Act 2, Scene 2 [Scene 3 of entire play], the Land of Memory, outside the house of Gaffer and Granny Tyl. Tyltyl (Gladys Hulette, behind table) and his sister Mytyl (Irene Brown, front), searching for the blue bird, come to the Land of Memory and have supper with their grandfather (Robert McWade, Sr.), their grandmother (Eleanor Carey) and their other brothers and sisters, all long dead. At the New Theatre, where the play was a decided success, this was Scene 4 of Act 1. The two girls dresed alike were the Fairbanks Twins, Marion and Madeline, who were later major performers in musical comedy and revue. This classic fantasy by Maeterlinck had its world premiere at the Moscow Art Theatre on Sept. 30, 1908. The English translation was first produced at the Haymarket, London, on Dec. 8, 1909. Paris was not to see *L'Oiseau bleu* until Mar. 2, 1911, five months after the New York premiere. (Photo: Byron)

1911

36
CHANTECLER, by Edmond Rostand (adapted by Louis N. Parker). Jan. 23, 1911. Knickerbocker Theatre. 96 perf. Prod.: Charles Frohman. Dir.: W. H. Gilmore. Sets: Ernest Gros, and J. M. & A. T. Hewlett & Charles Basing. Act 4 (set by Hewlett & Basing), the heart of the forest. The cock Chantecler (Maude Adams), scorned by the envious in his own barnyard, is persuaded by his beloved Hen Pheasant (May Blayney) to live with her in the forest. Here he receives noisome flattery from the Toads, who bear him no real love.

This forest set was acclaimed at the time as a revolution in stage scenery. The backdrops were merely black velvet curtains, the trees merely stenciled toned gauze; lighting did the rest. This boon to road companies was the invention of John W. Alexander, President of the National Academy of Design. *Chantecler* was first performed at the Théâtre de la Porte-Saint-Martin, Paris, on Feb. 7, 1910, with Lucien Guitry in the title role. (Photo: White)

1911

37

THE BOSS, by Edward Sheldon. Jan. 30, 1911. Astor Theatre. 88 perf. Prod. & supervised: Holbrook Blinn & William A. Brady. Dir.: Howard Estabrook. Sets: H. Robert Law. Act 2, the library of the contractor and political boss Michael Regan in a city on the Great Lakes (no doubt, Chicago). End of the act: Regan (Holbrook Blinn) rages against his wife Emily (Emily Stevens). Although she has married the uncouth Regan to save her father's business and protect the small depositors in his threatened banks, she has given support to Regan's enemies. After *Salvation Nell,* this play represented further progress in the careers of both playwright and leading man; it gave Blinn his first starring role. Emily Stevens was a younger cousin, protégée and pupil of Mrs. Fiske. (Photo: White)

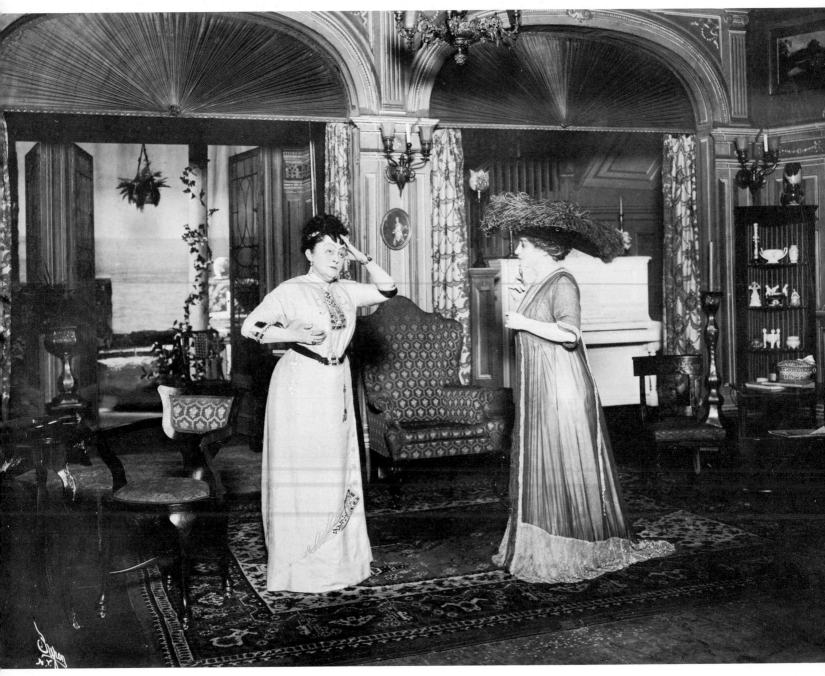

1911

38
MRS. BUMPSTEAD-LEIGH, by Harry James Smith. Apr. 3, 1911. Lyceum Theatre. 64 perf. Prod.: Harrison Grey Fiske. Dir.: Minnie Maddern Fiske & Harrison Grey Fiske. Set: D. Frank Dodge. The living room of a wealthy country house on Long Island. Act 1: Mrs. Bumpstead-Leigh (Mrs. Fiske), right, wife of an English clergyman, coaches her mother, Mrs. de Salle (Florine Arnold) in simulating an attack of vertigo in order to avoid a visitor who might unmask them as the Sayles family of Missionary Loop, Indiana, and thus spoil the marriage chances of the younger daughter. Here Mrs. Fiske had one of the most delightful comedy roles in all her years on the stage. (Photo: Byron)

1912

39
THE BIRD OF PARADISE, by Richard Walton Tully. Jan. 8, 1912. Daly's Theatre. 112 perf. Prod.: Oliver Morosco. Dir.: Richard Walton Tully. Sets: Ernest Gros. Act 1, a beach, cave and grass hut on the Puna Coast of the island of Hawaii in the early 1890s. The visiting American physician Paul Wilson (Lewis Stone) looks on as the native princess Luana (Laurette Taylor) asks the planter Captain Hatch (Theodore Roberts) to urge Wilson and his party to stay for a meal. The pouting girl, seated, right, is Mahumahu (Ida Waterman);

the old man, far right, is Hewahewa (Albert Perry); the other performers are native Hawaiians. This was the first play about Hawaii, a story of moral degeneration and rehabilitation in an exotic setting. The final scene included an eruption of Mount Kilauea. Californian in origin, *The Bird of Paradise* was first shown at Morosco's Belasco Theatre in Los Angeles on Sept. 11, 1911, and ran ten weeks there. Of the New York principals, only Lewis Stone was in the California production. (Photo: White)

1912

40
PEG O' MY HEART, by J. Hartley Manners. Dec. 20, 1912. Cort Theatre. 604 perf. Prod.: Oliver Morosco. Dir.: J. Hartley Manners. A living room in an old Tudor house in Scarborough, England. Act 2: Peg, who has just kept her cousin Ethel Chichester from eloping with a married man, now covers for her in front of the rest of the family. Left to right: Ethel (Christine Norman), Peg (Laurette Taylor), Ethel's mother (Emelie Melville), Ethel's brother Alaric (Hassard Short), the footman Jarvis (Peter Bassett). *Peg o' My Heart,* the very first production at the Cort Theatre, was Laurette Taylor's first starring play and one of the pinnacles of her career. The playwright-director was her current husband. The popular song of the same name (1913) was inspired by the play. (Photo: White)

1913

41

A GOOD LITTLE DEVIL, by Rosemonde Gérard & Maurice Rostand, from the novel by Mme de Ségur (adapted by Austin Strong). Jan. 8, 1913. Republic Theatre. 133 perf. Prod. & dir.: David Belasco. Sets: Edward G. Unitt & Wickes. Costumes: Percy Anderson. Act 2, Juliet's garden in a Scottish village. Charles MacLance, the "good little devil" (Ernest Truex), has taken French leave of his boarding school in order to visit his childhood sweetheart Juliet (Mary Pickford), whom he has not seen for two years. They are watched over solicitously by fairies invisible to them; the fairy immediately behind Juliet is Morgane (Lillian Gish). Pickford and Gish had already started making movies (in 1909 and 1912, respectively); Mary Pickford had worked for Belasco before, and it was he who gave her that stage name. The playwrights of *A Good Little Devil* were the wife and son of Edmond Rostand, author of *Cyrano* and *Chantecler*. The original French version, *Un bon petit diable,* was premiered at the Théâtre du Gymnase, Paris, on Dec. 22, 1911. (Photo: White)

1915

42
VERY GOOD EDDIE, by Philip Bartholomae & Guy Bolton (from Bartholomae's 1911 stage farce *Over Night*); lyrics by Schuyler Green; music by Jerome Kern. Dec. 22, 1915. Princess Theatre. 341 perf. Prod.: Marbury-Comstock Co. Gowns: Melville Ellis. Act 2, Scene 2, the Rip Van Winkle Inn on the Hudson. The girls of the chorus perform the "Fashion Show" number. *Very Good Eddie* was one of the bright, clever, forward-looking intimate musicals Kern and his associates put on at the Princess Theatre in the 1910s. (Perhaps this photo was taken at the Casino Theatre, to which the highly successful show moved in May 1916; at the Casino the director was Frank McCormack, the dances were arranged by David Bennett, and the Act 2 set was by Elsie de Wolfe—later Lady Mendl.) (Photo: White)

1917

43

IN THE ZONE, by Eugene O'Neill. Oct. 31, 1917 (season ended Apr. 27, 1918). Comedy Theatre. Performed in repertory with other one-act plays. Prod.: The Washington Square Players. The seamen's forecastle of the British tramp steamer *Glencairn.* Suspicious of the movements of one of the men—Smitty, the "Duke" (it is 1915 and the ship, laden with ammunition, is in the war zone)—his comrades tie him up and examine the black box he has been secreting. Left to right: Davis (Robert Strange), Smitty (Frederick Roland), Yank (Jay Strong), Driscoll (Arthur E. Hohl), Cocky (Rienzi de Cordova) and Scotty (Eugene Lincoln). O'Neill's one-act plays of the sea, based on his own experiences, were important in their own right and as building blocks for his full-length dramas. (Photo: White)

1917

44

THE LONG VOYAGE HOME, by Eugene O'Neill. Nov. 2, 1917. Playwright's Theatre. Performed in repertory with other one-act plays. Prod.: The Provincetown Players. Dir.: Nina Moise. Set: Ira Remson. A saloon on the Thames waterfront. The sailor Olson (Ira Remson), who has made enough money on the *Glencairn* to leave the sea and buy farm land in Sweden, is drugged and "crimped" (shanghaied). The whore Freda (Ida Rauh) hands his money to the saloonkeeper Fat Joe (George Cram Cook). Cook, himself a playwright and husband of the playwright Susan Glaspell, was one of the founders and directors of the Provincetown Players. (Photo: Paul Thompson)

1919

45

THE GODS OF THE MOUNTAIN, by Lord Dunsany. Repertory season started Jan. 15, 1919. Punch and Judy Theatre. Performed in repertory with other one-act plays. Prod.: Stuart Walker's Portmanteau Theatre. Dir.: Stuart Walker. Sets & costumes: Frank J. Zimmerer. Act [Scene] 2, the Metropolitan Hall of the city of Kongros. The beggar Agmar (Stuart Walker, with outstretched arm) and six other beggars, pretending to be the seven Gods of the Mountain, terrorize the citizenry. *The Gods of the Mountain* was first produced at the Haymarket, London, on June 1, 1911. Stuart Walker, an important pioneer in the little-theatre and repertory movements, gave it its first American production at Mount Holyoke, Mass., on Oct. 27, 1916, and its first New York production on Nov. 27, 1916, at the 39th Street Theatre. (Photo: White)

1919

46

THE JEST, by Sem Benelli (adapted by Edward Sheldon from the Italian, *La cena delle beffe*). Apr. 9, 1919. Plymouth Theatre. 77 perf. to end of season, then ran from Sept. 19 through Feb. 28, 1920. Prod & dir.: Arthur Hopkins. Sets. Robert Edmond Jones. John Barrymore's costumes by Maurice Herrmann, all others by Mme E. S. Freisinger. Act 1, the great hall in Tornaquinci's house in Florence, during the reign of Lorenzo the Magnificent. At a dinner party, the brutal Pisan captain of mercenaries Neri Chiaramentesi (Lionel Barry-more), with his mistress Ginevra (Maude Hanaford) at his feet, speaks insolently to the painter Giannetto Malespini (John Barrymore)—who is plotting revenge against him for cruel injuries—and to the host, Tornaquinci (Arthur Forrest). *The Jest* was a tremendous critical success. John Barrymore's association with Hopkins and Jones continued with his famous *Richard III* in 1920 and *Hamlet* in 1922. Benelli's play was originally produced at the Teatro Argentina, Rome, on Apr. 16, 1909. (Photo: Alfred Cheney Johnston)

47
JOHN FERGUSON, by St. John Ervine. May 13, 1919. Garrick Theatre. 177 perf. Prod.: The Theatre Guild. Dir.: Augustin Duncan. Set: Rollo Peters. Kitchen of John Ferguson's farmhouse in County Down in the 1880s. Act 3: James Caesar, in love with Ferguson's daughter Hannah, is arrested by Sergeant Kernaghan on suspicion of murdering the landlord who molested her. Left to right: the beggar "Clutie" John Magrath (Henry Herbert); John Ferguson (Augustin Duncan); his wife Sarah (Helen Westley); Hannah (Helen Freeman); Caesar (Dudley Digges); Kernaghan (Michael Carr); Andrew Ferguson (Rollo Peters), Hannah's brother and the real killer. The success of this second production of The Theatre Guild in its first season saved it from financial disaster; the young Walter Wanger acted as business manager for the show. The world premiere of the play was at the Abbey Theatre, Dublin, on Nov. 30, 1915.

1919

48
THE GOLD DIGGERS, by Avery Hopwood. Sept. 30, 1919. Lyceum Theatre. 720 perf. Prod. & dir.: David Belasco. Set: Ernest Gros. Dresses by Bendel. Jerry Lamar's apartment in New York City. Act 2: a tête-à-tête after a party; the once stuffy Stephen Lee (Bruce McRae) thinks Jerry Lamar (Ina Claire) is the actress from whose clutches he originally wanted to save his nephew. He now finds all her extravagances charming even when she pretends to be drunk and tells him tall tales of her scandalous past. This long-running, knowledgeable comedy about show girls was the fountainhead of countless plays and films on the subject. (Photo: White)

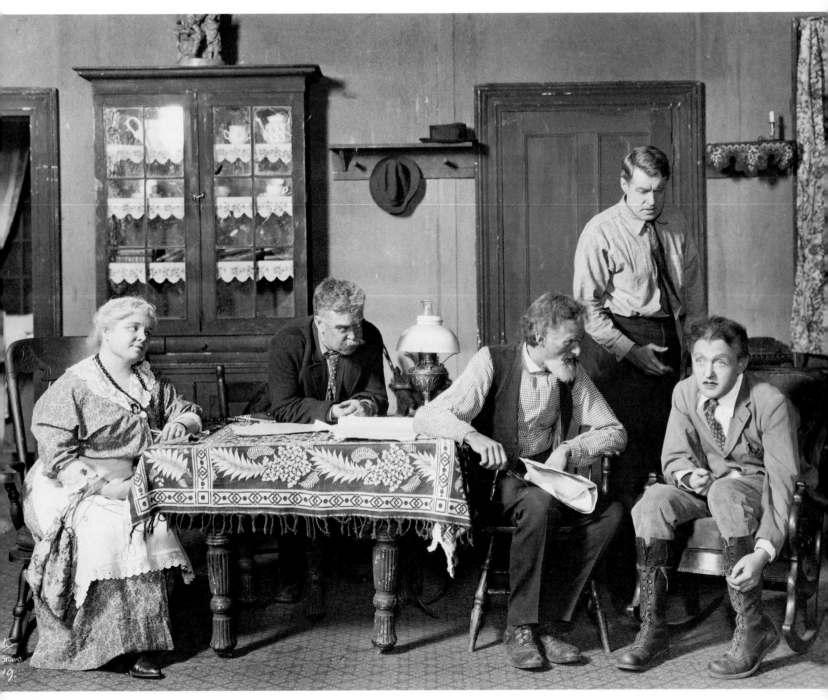

1920

49
BEYOND THE HORIZON, by Eugene O'Neill. Feb. 2, 1920. Morosco Theatre. 111 perf. Prod.: John D. Williams. Dir.: Homer Saint-Gaudens. Sets: Hewlett & Basing. Act 1, Scene 2, the sitting room of the Mayo farmhouse. Robert Mayo tells his family that he will not go to sea with his uncle as planned because he is in love (with a girl whom his brother Andrew loves, too). Left to right: Mrs. Kate Mayo (Mary Jeffery); her brother, Captain Dick Scott (Sidney Macy); Robert's father, James Mayo (Erville Alderson); Andrew (Robert Kelly); and Robert (Richard Bennett). O'Neill's first full-length play, also his first Broadway production, *Beyond the Horizon* won him the 1919/20 Pulitzer Prize and unprecedented critical acclaim as author of a true American tragedy. (Photo: White)

50

THE EMPEROR JONES, by Eugene O'Neill. Nov. 1, 1920. Provincetown Playhouse. 204 perf. Prod.: The Provincetown Players. Dir.: George Cram Cook. Set: Cleon Throckmorton. An island in the West Indies. Scene 4, Jones's vision of the road-gang episode in his past. As deposed emperor Brutus Jones escapes through the forest, he has visions of the fearful moments in his own past life and in the history of the Black race. The difference in the handling of the stage in the two O'Neill plays of 1920, *Beyond the Horizon* and *The Emperor Jones,* is striking; it is largely the difference between Broadway routine and new avant-garde talent, though the contrast in subject matter, plot structure and dialogue was a determining factor as well. (Photo: Vandamm)

1920

51
THE EMPEROR JONES. Scene 7, the atavistic vision of the Congo witch doctor (Iden Thompson) and the crocodile god. Jones (Charles S. Gilpin) is in the foreground. Gilpin was the first professional hired by the Provincetown group. The silhouette effects were aided by the first plaster cyclorama installed in a New York theater. (Photo: Vandamm)

1920

52
HEARTBREAK HOUSE, by George Bernard Shaw. Nov. 10, 1920. Garrick Theatre. 125 perf. Prod.: The Theatre Guild. Dir.: Dudley Digges. Sets: Lee Simonson. Act 3, the garden of Captain Shotover's house in Sussex. The house party is upset by a sudden bombardment that puts them in mind of Judgment Day. Left to right: Lady Ariadne Utterword (Lucile Watson), a daughter of the Captain; Hector Hushabye (Fred Eric), who dresses like an Arab to gratify his wife's whim; his wife Hesione (Effie Shannon), the Captain's other daughter; Ellie Dunn, a house guest (Elizabeth Risdon); Captain Shotover (Albert Perry). This was the world premiere of the monumental play. (Photo: Francis Bruguière)

1920

53
MISS LULU BETT, by Zona Gale (from her own novel). Dec. 27, 1920. Belmont Theatre. 176 perf. Prod. & dir.: Brock Pemberton. Sets: Sheldon K. Viele. Act 2, Scene 3, the side porch of the Deacon home. The fatuous Deacons return home in time to prevent their spoiled but disgusted daughter Di from eloping with young Bobby Larkin. Left to right: Mrs. Bett (Louise Closser Hale), mother of Ina and Lulu; Bobby (Jack Bohn); Mrs. Ina Deacon (Catherine Calhoun-Doucet);

Dwight Deacon (William E. Holden); Di (Beth Varden); and Lulu Bett (Carroll McComas), Ina's sister, who may or may not be married to Dwight's brother. This play, which won the Pulitzer Prize for the 1920/21 season, was performed at Sing Sing, on the night before its New York opening, on a collapsible stage donated to the prison by Belasco. After a week in New York, the third act was changed to make the ending happy instead of uncertain. (Photo: White)

1921

54

LILIOM, by Ferenc Molnár (translated from the Hungarian by Benjamin F. Glazer). Apr. 20, 1921. Garrick Theatre. 300 perf. Prod.: The Theatre Guild. Dir.: Frank Reicher. Sets & costumes: Lee Simonson. Scene 7, outside Julie's poor dwelling. Liliom (Joseph Schildkraut), allowed to return to earth for one day sixteen years after his death in order to do a good deed, visits his wife Julie (Eva Le Gallienne) and his daughter Louise (Evelyn Chard) in the guise of a beggar. When the Theatre Guild invited Schildkraut to act for them, on the recommendation of Kenneth Macgowan, the young actor insisted on *Liliom* as his play and Eva Le Gallienne as his leading lady (she had once nearly acted in an earlier translation of it called *The Daisy,* but it was never produced). Arthur Hopkins had been considering the play for John Barrymore, but released it. The success of both play and leading actors was enormous. *Liliom* was originally produced in Budapest in 1909. It was later used as the basis for the musical *Carousel.* (Photo: Francis Bruguière)

1921

55
KIKI, by André Picard (adapted from the French by David Belasco). Nov. 29, 1921. Belasco Theatre. 600 perf. Prod. & dir.: David Belasco. Sets: Ernest Gros. Act 2, the drawing room in the apartment of Victor Renal, manager of the "Folies Monplaisir" music hall. The amorous old Baron Rapp (Max Figman), a stockholder in the music hall, and Renal (Sam B. Hardy) observe the results of a tussle between Renal's cocky servant Adolphe (Thomas Mitchell) and Kiki (Lenore Ulric), a waif from the chorus whom Renal has taken home with him. *Kiki* had the longest New York run of any play adapted from the French. Its world premiere was at the Théâtre Edouard VII, Paris, Feb. 5, 1918. (Photo: White)

1922

56

HE WHO GETS SLAPPED, by Leonid Andreyev (translated from the Russian by Gregory Zilboorg). Jan. 9, 1922. Garrick Theatre. 308 perf. Prod.: The Theatre Guild. Dir.: Robert Milton. Set & costumes: Lee Simonson. A room off the ring of Briquet's Circus in a French city. Act 4: the equestrienne Consuelo (Margalo Gillmore), just before giving her farewell performance, enters on the arm of Baron Regnard (Louis Calvert), whom she intends to marry. Just below them on the stairs is "He" (Richard Bennett, in the polka-dot suit), a gentleman whose misfortunes have made him abandon his identity and become a clown. Playing the pipes are the clowns Tilly (Philip Leigh) and Polly (Edgar Stehli). The original Russian play, *Tot, kto polučaet poščečiny,* was first produced at the Dramatic Theatre, Moscow, in 1915. The translator, Zilboorg, later gained fame as a psychiatrist. (Photo: Vandamm)

1922

57
BACK TO METHUSELAH, by George Bernard Shaw. Presented in three parts on Feb. 27, Mar. 6 & Mar. 13, 1922. Garrick Theatre. 25 perf. Prod.: The Theatre Guild & the Neighborhood Playhouse. Dir.: Alice Lewisohn & Agnes Morgan; Frank Reicher; Philip Moeller. Sets & costumes: Lee Simonson. Third Cycle [Part 5, "As Far As Thought Can Reach"; directed by Moeller], a sunlit glade at the foot of a hill, with temple, grove and altar; the year is 31,920 A.D. The sculptor Arjillax (Stanley Howlett), standing on the altar, describes Michelangelo's Sistine ceiling as though it were an ancient fable; the newly hatched Amaryllis (Martha-Bryan Allen) listens with rapt attention. Two prestigious New York producing organizations joined forces to mount the world premiere of this vast philosophic opus. (Photo: Vandamm)

1922

58
THE HAIRY APE, by Eugene O'Neill. Mar. 9, 1922. Province-town Playhouse. Prod.: The Provincetown Players. Dir.: James Light. Sets: Robert Edmond Jones & Cleon Throckmorton. Scene 1, the firemen's forecastle of a transatlantic liner. Robert Smith, known as Yank (Louis Wolheim), tells his colleagues that he as a stoker represents the positive, forward-looking life force of contemporary civilization. In this play O'Neill transmuted some of the characters, themes and even dialogue of his earlier, romantically naturalistic, one-acters of the sea into an expressionistic frenzy that was matched by the settings. (Photo: Vandamm)

1922

59
THE HAIRY APE. Scene 5, a Sunday morning on Fifth Avenue in the Fifties, where Yank has come to see the capitalist class in its natural habitat. Josephine Hutchinson and George Tobias were among the bit players in this production. (Photo: Vandamm)

60
GREENWICH VILLAGE FOLLIES OF 1922, book by George V. Hobart; lyrics by Irving Caesar & John Murray Anderson; music by Louis A. Hirsch. Sept. 19, 1922. Shubert Theatre. 216 perf. Prod.: Bohemians, Inc. Dir.: John Murray Anderson (dance direction by Carl Randall & Alexander Yakovleff). Set & costumes for "The Nights": Howard Greer. Part [Act] 2, Scene 9, the cast line-up of the "Nights" finale (in the center are the stars of this fourth annual edition, the female im-personator Bert Savoy and his partner Jay Brennan; second from the extreme left is Carl Randall; in the dark dress with the high white collar is the French chanteuse Yvonne George). The finale celebrated the heady night life of many cosmopolitan centers, with Greenwich Village Nights as the climax. A sketch on advertising slogans written by George S. Kaufman was another feature of this 1922 edition. (Photo: Abbe)

1922

61
R.U.R. (Rossum's Universal Robots), by Karel Čapek (translated from the Czech by Paul Selver & Nigel Playfair). Oct. 9, 1922. Garrick Theatre. 184 perf. Prod.: The Theatre Guild. Dir.: Philip Moeller. Sets & costumes: Lee Simonson. Act 3, the drawing room in Helena and Domin's home on the island where the Robots are manufactured. A group of rebellious Robots, led by the especially intelligent Radius (John Rutherford), formerly of the household, break into the room, bent on destruction. This threatening glance into a depersonalized future added the word "robot" to our language. *R.U.R.* was originally produced in Prague on Jan. 26, 1921. (Photo: Vandamm)

1923

62
SUN UP, by Lula Vollmer. May 24, 1923. Provincetown Playhouse. 356 perf. Prod.: Players Company, Inc., by arrangement with Lee Kugel. Dir.: Henry Stillman & Benjamin Kauser. Set: Oscar Liebetrau. The interior of Widow Cagle's cabin near Asheville, North Carolina, 1918. Act 3, Scene 2: Mrs. Cagle, about to shoot the Army deserter (right) who has been revealed as the son of the revenuer who killed her husband, hears the spirit voice of her son killed in the war urging her to forgive. Left to right: Mrs. Cagle (Lucille LaVerne); a neighbor's son, Bud Todd (Gene Lockhart); Emmy, Bud's sister and Mrs. Cagle's daughter-in-law (Anne Elstner); the deserter, Zeb Turner (Elliott Cabot). This was an outstanding early example of the full-length folk play. (Photo: White)

1923

63
THE SWAN, by Ferenc Molnár (translated by Melville Baker from the Hungarian, *A Hattyu*). Oct. 23, 1923. Cort Theatre. 255 perf. Prod.: Charles Frohman Co. Dir.: David Burton. Sets for Acts 1 & 3: Herman Rosse. Eva Le Gallienne's dresses by Molyneux, Paris. Act 1, Princess Beatrice's castle in Hungary; a garden pavilion that serves as a classroom for her sons. Princess Beatrice comes to see how the boys are doing and to tell them of the arrival of her brother, Father Hyacinth. Left to right: Princess Alexandra (Eva Le Gallienne), daughter of Beatrice, betrothed to a royal heir-apparent; Beatrice (Hilda Spong); the boys, Arsen (George Walcott) and Georg (Alan Willey); and their tutor, in love with Alexandra, Dr. Hans Agi (Basil Rathbone). This modern classic was first performed in Budapest in 1920. (Photo: White)

1923

64
SAINT JOAN, by George Bernard Shaw. Dec. 28, 1923. Garrick Theatre. At least 195 perf. Prod.: The Theatre Guild. Dir.: Philip Moeller. Sets & costumes: Raymond Sovey. Act 4 (Scene 6 in text), a stone hall in the castle of Rouen arranged for a trial, May 30, 1431. When she learns that lifelong imprisonment awaits her even though she has signed a recantation of heresy, Joan (Winifred Lenihan) rips the paper and cries: "Light your fire!" In the judges' seats: the Inquisitor (Joseph Macaulay) and Bishop Cauchon (Ian Maclaren). This was the world premiere. (Photo: Francis Bruguière)

1924

65
HELL-BENT FER HEAVEN, by Hatcher Hughes. Jan. 4, 1924. Klaw Theatre. 122 perf. Prod.: Mark Klaw, Inc. Dir.: Augustin Duncan. Set: Sheldon K. Viele. The interior of the Hunt home in the Carolina mountains. Act 2: Andy Lowry (Glenn Anders), made drunk with home-distilled liquor, and fighting mad with talk of old feuds, by the shifty hired hand Rufe

Pryor, a religious fanatic, is determined to kill easy-going Sid Hunt (George Abbott), just back from the war in France and in love with Andy's sister. Andy forces Sid to dance while Rufe (John F. Hamilton) plays "Turkey in the Straw" on the banjo. Pulitzer Prize 1923/24. (Photo: White)

1924

66

THE MIRACLE (*Das Mirakel*), by Karl Vollmoeller. Jan. 16, 1924. Century Theatre. At least 175 perf. Prod.: F. Ray Comstock & Morris Gest (with Gest's personal supervision). Dir.: Max Reinhardt (special stage direction by Richard Boleslavsky). Sets, costumes & lighting: Norman Bel Geddes. Scene 2, a forest. The Nun Megildis (Rosamond Pinchot) mutely pleads for mercy from the Robber Count (Lionel Braham), whose huntsmen have overcome and bound the Knight (Orville Caldwell) with whom she ran away from the Cathedral.

This famous play without dialogue had an enormous cathedral setting, elements of which remained on stage in every scene. The role of the Nun in the New York production was played in rotation by Rosamond Pinchot and Lady Diana Manners (Lady Duff-Cooper). *The Miracle* was originally produced by Charles Cochran at Olympia (a sports arena) in London on Dec. 24, 1911. The background music was specially composed by Engelbert Humperdinck. (Photo: White)

BEGGAR ON HORSEBACK, by George S. Kaufman & Marc Connelly (suggested by the play *Hans Sonnenstössers Höllenfahrt* by Paul Apel). Feb. 12, 1924. Broadhurst Theatre. At least 144 perf. Prod. & dir.: Winthrop Ames. Sets & costumes: Woodman Thompson. Part [Act] 1: now that the penniless and overwrought young composer Neil McRae has proposed to a dull rich girl for financial security, his apartment, which had been the basic set, is blended in his dream with a railroad station where his wedding is performed. Left to right: ushers; the bride, Gladys Cady (Ann Carpenger); Neil (Roland Young); his friend Albert Rice, officiating as minister (Richard Barbee); a trainman; Mr. Cady, the bride's father (George Barbier); a trainboy; Homer Cady, the bride's obnoxious brother (Osgood Perkins); Mrs. Cady, the bride's mother (Marion Ballou); bandsmen. The wedding procession marched down two aisles past the audience and onto the stage. The background music, representing Neil's symphony and otherwise very important in establishing the various shifts from reality to fantasy, was by Deems Taylor. (Photo: White)

1924

68
THE GUARDSMAN, by Ferenc Molnár (translated by Grace I. Colbron & Hans Bartsch from the Hungarian, *A Testör*; acting version by Philip Moeller). Oct. 13, 1924. Garrick Theatre. 280 perf. Prod.: The Theatre Guild. Dir.: Philip Moeller. Sets: Jo Mielziner. Act 3, the living room in the Actor's home in Vienna. The Actor (Alfred Lunt) changes once more into the guise of the Russian Imperial guardsman which he had as-sumed previously to test the fidelity of his Actress wife (Lynn Fontanne). This was their first team-up in a regular production, and the first set assignment of 23-year-old Jo Mielziner. The play, originally produced in Budapest in 1910, had been presented earlier in the U.S. as *Where Ignorance Is Bliss* (1913).

69

DESIRE UNDER THE ELMS, by Eugene O'Neill. Nov. 11, 1924. Greenwich Village Theatre. At least 208 perf. Prod.: The Provincetown Players. Dir. & set: Robert Edmond Jones. The Cabot farmhouse, New England, 1850 (the set showed the exterior constantly, and any interiors that were needed for the scene). Part [Act] 2, Scene 2, the bedrooms upstairs. Old Ephraim Cabot (Walter Huston) yearns to have a son by his young new wife Abbie (Mary Morris), as she and Cabot's son Eben (Charles Ellis) gaze longingly in each other's direction through the partition separating the rooms. *Desire Under the Elms* had both the stark family tragedy and the dour New England setting that were to recur in O'Neill's work. (Photo: Vandamm)

1925

70
WILD BIRDS, by Dan Totheroh. Apr. 9, 1925. Cherry Lane Playhouse. 44 perf. Prod.: Cherry Lane Players, Inc. Dir.: John Wray. Sets: Joseph Mullen. Lighting: Frank Carrington. Act 3, Scene 2, Adam's room in the attic. Adam Larsen (Donald Duff) and Mazie (Mildred MacLeod) are two young loners whose love is shattered by their harsh environment of farm life on the prairies. *Wild Birds* was originally produced at the University of California's Greek Theatre at Berkeley about 1922, after winning first prize in a play contest judged by Eugene O'Neill, Susan Glaspell and George Jean Nathan. It was subsequently mounted by the semiprofessional Players' Club of San Francisco. The Cherry Lane engagement was its professional premiere, and it enjoyed a great *succès d'estime.* (Photo: Byron)

1925

71
CRAIG'S WIFE, by George Kelly. Oct. 12, 1925. Morosco Theatre. 360 perf. Prod.: Rosalie Stewart. Dir.: George Kelly. Set: Sheldon K. Viele. The living room of the Craig home. Act 2: Harriet Craig (Chrystal Herne) asks her housekeeper Mrs. Harold (Josephine Williams) and her maid Mazie (Mary Gildea) to find her husband, after she realizes that some of her meddling may have implicated her household in a murder just reported in the paper. The title character has become a byword for a selfish wife who considers her house physically sacrosanct. Pulitzer Prize 1925/26. (Photo: White)

1925

72

THE DYBBUK, by S. Ansky (adapted by Henry G. Alsberg from the Habima production). Dec. 15, 1925. The Neighborhood Playhouse. 120 perf. Prod.: The Neighborhood Playhouse. Dir.: David Vardi (in association with Alice Lewisohn). Sets & costumes: Aline Bernstein. Act 2, a square in Brainitz between Sender's house and the synagogue. On her return from a ritual visit to the graveyard just before her wedding, Leah (Mary Ellis) is found to be possessed by the spirit of the dead student of Kabbala who loved her. Left of her is the old woman Frade (Dorothy Sands); looking forward rigidly is the weak bridegroom Menashe (Harold Minjer).

This classic folk play was first performed in its original Yiddish (*Der Dibbuk*) in Warsaw by the Vilna Troupe on Dec. 9, 1920. Maurice Schwartz produced it at his Yiddish Art Theatre in New York in 1921. The Neighborhood Playhouse production, the first in English, was based on the Hebrew-language version of the Moscow Habima group, which had not yet come to New York. The singer Mary Ellis, who had created the role of Rose-Marie in Friml's operetta, was doing straight drama while resting her singing voice from a strain. (Photo: Francis Bruguière)

1926

73
THE GREAT GOD BROWN, by Eugene O'Neill. Jan. 23, 1926. Greenwich Village Theatre. 271 perf. Prod.: Kenneth Macgowan, Robert Edmond Jones & Eugene O'Neill. Dir. & sets: Robert Edmond Jones. Masks: William Stahl & James Light. Act 4, Scene 2, the library of William Brown's home. The earth-mother courtesan Cybel (Ann Shoemaker) comes to warn Brown (William Harrigan) that he is being pursued for murdering himself (after the death of his friend/rival Dion Anthony, he had assumed Anthony's persona and had made it seem that Anthony had done away with Brown). In this interesting play O'Neill used masks to exteriorize conflicts between and within personalities. (Photo: Vandamm)

1926

74
LULU BELLE, by Edward Sheldon & Charles MacArthur. Feb. 9, 1926. Belasco Theatre. 461 perf. Prod. & dir.: David Belasco. Sets: Joseph Wickes' Studio. Act 1, the sidewalks of the downtown New York Black neighborhood, San Juan Hill (the script specifies West 59th Street). The trollop Lulu Belle (Lenore Ulric, in the dark dress) has a tiff with another girl, Ruby Lee (Evelyn Preer), who has accused her of man-stealing. This elaborate production, an up-to-date Black version of the Carmen and Don José plot (already!), had about 100 Black performers in addition to fifteen Whites, but the latter had all the main roles. Branded as indecent by some critics, the play (MacArthur's first) made a great impact on the public mind. "Lulu Belle" became a generic term for a Harlem floozy, as in the lyrics of Irving Berlin's song "Puttin' On the Ritz." Gershwin, already on the lookout for an opera subject based on Black life, considered *Lulu Belle* until *Porgy* made its striking appearance. (Photo: White)

1926

75
THE GARRICK GAIETIES, sketches by Benjamin M. Kaye, Newman Levy & others; lyrics by Lorenz Hart; music by Richard Rodgers. May 10, 1926. Garrick Theatre. 174 perf. Prod.: The Theatre Guild. Dir.: Philip Loeb (musical numbers arranged by Herbert Fields). Sets & costumes: Carolyn Hancock. This was the opening number, "Six Little Plays," spoofing recent Theatre Guild productions. Left to right: *Arms and the Man* (Betty Starbuck); *Merchants of Glory* (Jack Edwards); *Goat Song* (William Griffith); *The Garrick Gaieties* (Sterling Holloway); a mortician (Philip Loeb); *The Chief Thing* (Edith Meiser); *Androcles and the Lion* (Romney Brent) and *The Glass Slipper* (Blanche Fleming). This was the second edition of *The Garrick Gaieties,* the one with the song "Mountain Greenery." (Photo: Drix Duryea)

1926

76
BROADWAY, by Philip Dunning & George Abbott. Sept. 16, 1926. Broadhurst Theatre. 603 perf. Prod.: Jed Harris. Dir.: Philip Dunning & George Abbott. Set: Arthur P. Segal. The private party room of the Paradise nightclub. Act 2: the showgirl Pearl (Eloise Stream) faints when she hears that her gangster sweetheart has been killed; the actual killer, Steve Crandall (Robert Gleckler), and some of his henchmen, unaware of her connection with the victim, look on with solicitude. The combination of melodrama and hoofing, gang wars and backstage billingsgate, made this play unusually successful and a strong influence on stage and screen for years. (Photo: White)

1926

77
THE PLAY'S THE THING, by Ferenc Molnár (adapted by P. G. Wodehouse). Nov. 3, 1926. Henry Miller's Theatre. 326 perf. Prod.: Charles Frohman Co. Dir.: Holbrook Blinn. A room in a castle on the Italian Riviera. Act 2: in order to save his young composer's marriage, and thus their forthcoming operetta, the crafty librettist Sandor Turai (Holbrook Blinn) orders the fiancée, Ilona Szabo (Catherine Dale Owen), and her former lover, the actor Almady (Reginald Owen), to declare that the love scene between them overheard the night before by the composer was a play rehearsal. The original Hungarian play, *Játék a Kastélyban* (literally "A Play in the Castle"), was first produced in Budapest in 1925. (Photo: Vandamm)

1926

78
NED McCOBB'S DAUGHTER, by Sidney Howard. Nov. 22, 1926. John Golden Theatre. 156 perf. Prod.: The Theatre Guild. Dir.: Philip Moeller. Sets: Aline Bernstein. Act 1, "Carrie's Spa," an eating place next to a Maine ferry terminus. Left to right: Babe Callahan, Carrie's bootlegger brother-in-law (Alfred Lunt); a Federal man on the lookout for local bootleggers (Maurice McRae); the waitress Jenny (Margalo Gillmore); another Federal man (Morris Carnovsky); George Callahan, Carrie's husband, who works on the ferry (Earle Larimore); Ned McCobb, Carrie's father, who runs the ferry (Albert Perry); and Carrie (Clare Eames, the playwright's wife). This particular grouping of characters does not occur in the course of the play. *Ned McCobb's Daughter* and the following play, *The Silver Cord,* also by Howard, played in repertory at the John Golden Theatre in the winter of 1926/27. (Photo: Vandamm)

1926

79
THE SILVER CORD, by Sidney Howard. Dec. 20, 1926. John Golden Theatre. 112 perf. Prod.: The Theatre Guild. Dir.: John Cromwell. Sets: Cleon Throckmorton, Inc. Laura Hope Crews's gowns by Henri Bendel. Act 3, the living room of Mrs. Phelps's home. About to leave her mother-in-law's house, Christina tells Hester, the jilted fiancée of her spineless brother-in-law Robert Phelps, that her own husband David will not cleave to her but will remain behind as his mother's plaything. Left to right: Robert (Earle Larimore), Christina (Elizabeth Risdon), Hester (Margalo Gillmore), David (Elliott Cabot), Mrs. Phelps (Laura Hope Crews). This was the archetypical dissection of the abnormally possessive mother. (Photo: Vandamm)

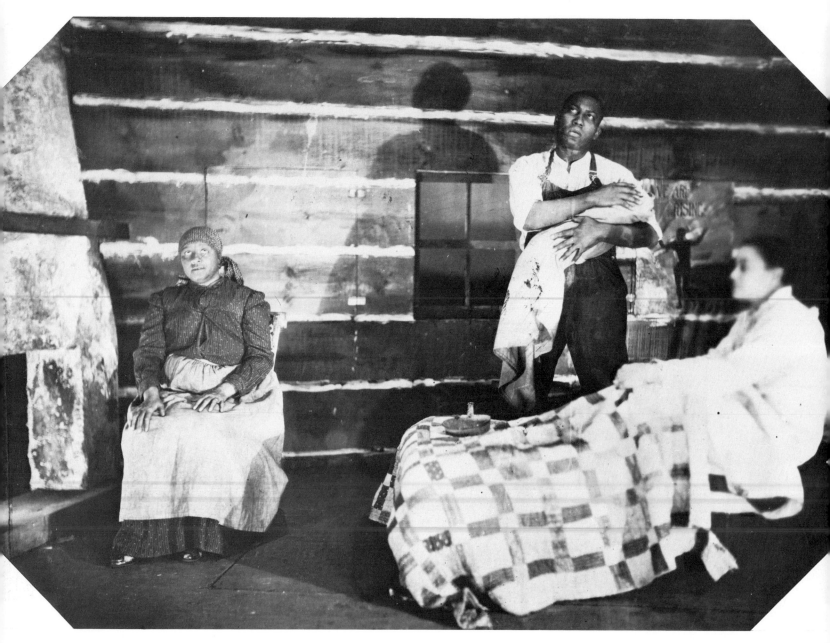

1926

80
IN ABRAHAM'S BOSOM, by Paul Green. Dec. 30, 1926. Provincetown Playhouse. 200 perf. Prod.: The Provincetown Players. Dir.: Jasper Deeter. Sets: Cleon Throckmorton. Costumes: Evelyn Clifton. Scene 2, Abraham McCranie's cabin in eastern North Carolina, 1888. Abraham (Julius Bledsoe), elated at the thought of being able to teach school at last, takes new joy in his infant son and looks forward to a bright future. With him are his aunt, Muh Mack (Abbie Mitchell), and his wife Goldie (Rose McClendon). Produced on a shoestring, this was the first full-length play by Green, who had contributed several excellent one-acters to the little-theater and folk-play movements. Pulitzer Prize 1926/27.

1927

81
THE CRADLE SONG, by Gregorio & María Martínez Sierra (translated from the Spanish, *Canción de cuna,* by John Garrett Underhill). Jan. 24, 1927. Civic Repertory Theatre. 57 perf. Prod.: Civic Repertory Theatre. Dir.: Eva Le Gallienne. Sets & costumes: Gladys E. Calthrop. End of Act 1, a room opening on the cloister of a Dominican convent in Spain.

The homesick young novice Sister Joanna of the Cross (Eva Le Gallienne) feels a strong maternal attraction toward the foundling just adopted by the convent. Originally produced at the Teatro Lara, Madrid, in 1911, this bittersweet comedy had also had some special matinee performances in New York in 1921, directed by Augustin Duncan. (Photo: White)

1927

82
SATURDAY'S CHILDREN, by Maxwell Anderson. Jan. 26, 1927. Booth Theatre. 310 perf. Prod.: Actors' Theatre, Inc. Dir.: Guthrie McClintic. Act 2, the kitchen-dining room of the O'Neil apartment. Bobby O'Neil (Ruth Gordon), whose existence as a young wife in an impecunious household is full of thorns, rejects the cheap scheming of her older sister Florrie (Ruth Hammond) but can only look forward to flippancy from her father, Mr. Halevy (Frederick Perry). This was the first solo success of Maxwell Anderson, who had collaborated with Laurence Stallings on *What Price Glory?* in 1924.

1927

83
THE SECOND MAN, by S. N. Behrman. Apr. 11, 1927. Guild Theatre. 44 perf. Prod.: The Theatre Guild. Dir.: Philip Moeller. Set: Jo Mielziner. Margalo Gillmore's dress by Hattie Carnegie. The living room of Clark Storey's suite in a studio building on the West Side. Act 2, Scene 2, the champagne party. Left to right: Kendall Frayne (Lynn Fontanne), the wealthy socialite who supports Storey financially but cannot decide whether or not to marry him; Storey (Alfred Lunt), the writer of slick magazine fiction who has a cynical "second man" inside him mocking his natural impulses; Monica Grey (Margalo Gillmore), in love with Storey and wooed by the rich but unworldly research chemist Austin Lowe; Lowe (Earle Larimore). This was Behrman's first success, and one of his finest efforts. (Photo: Vandamm)

1927

84

THE FIELD GOD, by Paul Green. Apr. 20, 1927. Greenwich Village Theatre. 45 perf. Prod. & dir.: Edwin R. Wolfe. Sets: Louis Bromberg. Act 2, Scene 1, the back yard and rear part of the Gilchrist farmhouse in eastern North Carolina, about 1904. Hardy Gilchrist grapples with his young hired hand Neill Sykes, who has attacked him out of jealousy: both are attracted to Rhoda Campbell, Mrs. Gilchrist's young niece who has come to live in the house. Left to right: Jacob Alford, a farm helper (Arthur Allen); Sion Alford, his son (Claudius Mintz); Etta Gilchrist, Hardy's wife (Adelaide Fitz-Allen); Lonie (Lillie Brayton) and Mag (Clara Thropp), day laborers; Rhoda (Ruth Mason); Neill (Ben Smith); and Hardy (Fritz Leiber). Religious tolerance was also a major theme of this play. (Photo: Vandamm)

1927

85
PORGY, by Dorothy & Du Bose Heyward (from his novel). Oct. 10, 1927. Guild Theatre. 367 perf. Prod.: The Theatre Guild. Dir.: Rouben Mamoulian. Sets: Cleon Throckmorton. Act 2, Scene 4, Serena's room in Catfish Row, Charleston. Crown (Jack Carter) rushes out into the storm to save Clara, who has gone out to find her husband, the fisherman Jake. One of the greatest American plays and most memorable productions of the twentieth century, *Porgy* was, of course, the basis of Gershwin's 1935 opera *Porgy and Bess*. (Photo: Vandamm)

1927

86
THE PLOUGH AND THE STARS, by Sean O'Casey. Nov. 28, 1927. Hudson Theatre. 32 perf. Prod.: George C. Tyler. Dir.: Tony Quinn. Act 3, the street outside a Dublin slum tenement during the Easter Week uprising in 1916. As the mordantly pro-British Bessie Burgess (Sara Allgood) watches from her window, Irish Captain Brennan (Edwin Elliss) comforts the wounded Lieutenant Langon (Tony Quinn), and Nora Clitheroe (Shelah Richards) rushes out of the building to embrace her husband Jack (Michael Scott) and urge him to leave the fighting. This first American production was performed by the Irish Players. The world premiere was at the Abbey Theatre, Dublin, on Feb. 8, 1926.

1927

87

THE ROYAL FAMILY, by George S. Kaufman & Edna Ferber. Dec. 28, 1927. Selwyn Theatre. 345 perf. Prod.: Jed Harris. Dir.: David Burton. Set: James Reynolds. A duplex apartment in the East Fifties. Act 3: Tony, the madcap Hollywood star among the Cavendish dynasty of actors, returns unexpectedly from abroad with an Indian servant and a small menagerie. Left to right: Tony's sister, Julie Cavendish (Ann Andrews); Gilbert Marshall (Joseph King); Jo the houseman (Royal C. Stout); two hall boys (Wally Stuart & Lester Niel-son); Gunga (Hubert Courtney); Della the maid (Josephine Williams); Tony (Otto Kruger); his mother, Fanny Cavendish (Haidée Wright); her brother, Herbert Dean (Orlando Daly); his wife Kitty (Catherine Calhoun-Doucet); the producer Oscar Wolfe (Jefferson De Angelis); and Julie's daughter Gwen (Sylvia Field). One of show business' frequent paeans to itself, this comedy was suggested by some of the traditions and escapades of the Drew-Barrymore clan. (Photo: White)

1928

88

MARCO MILLIONS, by Eugene O'Neill. Jan. 9, 1928. Guild Theatre. 92 perf. Prod.: The Theatre Guild. Dir.: Rouben Mamoulian. Sets & costumes: Lee Simonson. Act 2, Scene 3, the poop deck of the royal junk of the Princess Kukachin at anchor in the harbor of Hormuz, Persia. As his father Nicolo (Henry Travers) and his uncle Maffeo (Ernest Cossart) count their money, Marco Polo (Alfred Lunt), who has commanded the ship bearing Kublai's granddaughter Kukachin (Margalo Gillmore) from China to wed the King of Persia, informs her that the intended bridegroom has died during their journey and that she is to marry his son and heir instead. This was a semipermanent setting, with the upstage framework altered in details to indicate various locales. It is staggering to reflect that this exotic O'Neill satire was produced by the Guild in the same month that they introduced the mammoth *Strange Interlude*. (Photo: Vandamm)

1928

89
STRANGE INTERLUDE, by Eugene O'Neill. Jan. 30, 1928. John Golden Theatre. 426 perf. Prod.: The Theatre Guild. Dir.: Philip Moeller. Sets: Jo Mielziner. Act 7, the sitting room of the Evans' apartment on Park Avenue. Nina Leeds Evans (Lynn Fontanne), who has had a child by a man other than her husband because of the threat of inherited insanity, is dismayed at the hatred her son Gordon (Charles Walters) feels for his (unsuspected) real father Edmund Darrell (Glenn Anders). This, of course, was the play celebrated for the spoken stream-of-consciousness of all the characters, including the eleven-year-old boy. There were nine acts, with a one-hour dinner intermission after Act 5. Pulitzer Prize 1927/28. O'Neill originally imagined Katharine Cornell in the role of Nina. (Photo: Vandamm)

1928

90
THE THREE MUSKETEERS, by William Anthony McGuire; lyrics by P. G. Wodehouse & Clifford Grey; music by Rudolf Friml (based on the novel *Les trois mousquetaires* by Alexandre Dumas *père).* Mar. 13, 1928. Lyric Theatre. 318 perf. Prod.: Florenz Ziegfeld. Dir.: William Anthony McGuire (dance direction by Albertina Rasch, ensembles directed by Richard Boleslavsky). Sets: Joseph Urban. Costumes: John Harkrider. Act 2, Scene 5, the ballroom of the Hôtel de Ville, Paris. This is musical number 27, the "Ballet of the King," performed by Harriet Hoctor and the Albertina Rasch Girls. It is at this ball that the Queen is supposed to wear the diamond heart which Richelieu knows she gave to the Duke of Buckingham! This is an example of the "luxury" in which Ziegfeld often indulged. The versatile Urban, also an architect, designed for the Follies and the Metropolitan Opera with equal aplomb. (Photo: White)

1928

91
THE FRONT PAGE, by Ben Hecht & Charles MacArthur. Aug. 14, 1928. Times Square Theatre. 276 perf. Prod.: Jed Harris. Dir.: George S. Kaufman. Set. Raymond Sovey. The press room in the Criminal Courts Building, Chicago, where reporters from many papers are covering a hanging. This does not seem to be any particular moment in the action, but a partial cast line-up. Among those present: (first white shirt from left) Murphy of the *Journal* (Willard Robertson), (center, at phone, with dark hat) Endicott of the *Post* (Allen Jenkins), (second white shirt) McCue of the News Bureau (William Foran), (at desk) Bensinger of the *Tribune* (Walter Baldwin). The lively setting and properties were used actively and constructively during the play, even the rolltop desk, which at one point concealed an escaped criminal. (Photo: Van-damm)

1928

92

THE CHERRY ORCHARD, by Anton Chekhov (translated from the Russian, *Vishnëvyi sad,* by Constance Garnett). Oct. 15, 1928. Civic Repertory Theatre. 63 perf. Prod.: Civic Repertory Theatre, Inc. Dir.: Eva Le Gallienne. Sets & costumes: Aline Bernstein. Act 1, the former nursery in the Ranevsky home. The presence of Petya Trofimov (Harold Moulton), who was the tutor of her dead son, reminds Madame Ranevsky (Alla Nazimova) of her loss. This was an especially distinguished revival of the masterwork originally produced at the Moscow Art Theatre on Jan. 17, 1904.

1929

93
STREET SCENE, by Elmer Rice. Jan. 10, 1929. Playhouse. 601 perf. Prod.: William A. Brady, Ltd. Dir.: Elmer Rice. Set: Jo Mielziner. The exterior of an apartment house in a mean quarter of New York. End of Act 2: Samuel Kaplan (Horace Braham) tries to comfort Rose Maurrant (Erin O'Brien-Moore) as she leans over her dying mother Anna (Mary Servoss), whose husband has shot her for infidelity. An actual house at 25 West 65th Street was duplicated for this famous setting. After numerous rejections by producers, and after walkouts by directors (Cukor and Mamoulian) once Brady had decided to gamble on the play, *Street Scene* went on to be a stunning success and to win the Pulitzer Prize for 1928/29. (Photo: White)

1929

94

DYNAMO, by Eugene O'Neill. Feb. 11, 1929. Martin Beck Theatre. 50 perf. Prod.: The Theatre Guild. Dir.: Philip Moeller. Sets: Lee Simonson. Act 1, Scene 1, through Act 2, Scene 2, the exterior of the homes of the Lights and the Fifes in a small Connecticut town, showing the antagonistic fathers, the Reverend Hutchins Light (George Gaul) and the atheistic hydroelectric plant superintendent Ramsay Fife (Dudley Digges). This does not correspond to any moment in the text. *Dynamo* used the cutaway houses of *Desire Under the Elms* and the spoken thoughts of *Strange Interlude,* but could not duplicate the success of the earlier plays. (Photo: Vandamm)

1929

95
DYNAMO. Act 3, Scene 3, the interiors of the dynamo and switchboard rooms in the plant. Mrs. May Fife (Catherine Calhoun-Doucet) and Reuben Light, the minister's son (Glenn Anders), are shown worshipping the dynamo. This does not occur in the action of the play. O'Neill prepared a working sketch of this set which was followed closely in the actual execution. The interesting cast included Claudette Colbert and, in a tiny role, Herbert J. Biberman. (Photo: Vandamm)

1930

96

THE GREEN PASTURES, by Marc Connelly (based on the book *Ol' Man Adam an' His Chillun* by Roark Bradford). Feb. 26, 1930. Mansfield Theatre. 640 perf. Prod.: Laurence Rivers. Dir.: Marc Connelly. Sets: Robert Edmond Jones. Part [Act] 2, Scene 3, Pharaoh's throne room. Moses (Alonzo Fenderson) and his brother Aaron (McKinley Reeves) perform little miracles before magic-loving Pharaoh (George Randol) to gain his sympathy for their urgent request—letting their people go. In this play, which presented the Bible stories in terms and settings familiar to Southern Blacks, Pharaoh's throne room took on the trappings of a lodge room. Pulitzer Prize 1929/30. (Photo: Vandamm)

1930

97
HOTEL UNIVERSE, by Philip Barry. Apr. 14, 1930. Martin Beck Theatre. 81 perf. Prod.: The Theatre Guild. Dir.: Philip Moeller. Set: Lee Simonson. Ladies' dresses by Saks–Fifth Avenue. Play in one scene, the terrace of Ann Field's house on the French Riviera. As the various house guests act out their compulsive illusions, the preternaturally wise Stephen Field (Morris Carnovsky) assumes the temporary role of the father of actress Lily Malone (Ruth Gordon), hoping to cure her of the fantasies connected with her childhood. This was an early example of a long drama without intermissions. (Photo: Vandamm)

1930

98
ONCE IN A LIFETIME, by Moss Hart & George S. Kaufman. Sept. 24, 1930. Music Box. 406 perf. Prod.: Sam H. Harris. Dir.: George S. Kaufman. Sets: Cirker & Robbins. Costumes: Eaves & others. Act 3, Scene 1, on the set of the Glogauer film studio in Hollywood: the filming of the wedding scene from *Gingham and Orchids.* Conducting the service is the film actor Jackson, playing the Bishop (Granville Bates); at the right is the German film director Rudolph Kammerling (Walter Dreher). This was a satire on the situation in Hollywood following the public acceptance of the Vitaphone. The principal characters are unemployed vaudevillians who pass themselves off as great speech experts from the East and fool the insecure movie mogul whose stars are not strong on elocution. (Photo: White)

1930

99
THREE'S A CROWD, by Howard Dietz; lyrics by Dietz & others; music by Arthur Schwartz & others. Oct. 15, 1930. Selwyn Theatre. 272 perf. Prod.: Max Gordon. Dir. & lighting: Hassard Short (dance direction by Albertina Rasch). Sets: Albert Johnson. Costumes: Kiviette. This was the "Something to Remember You By" number, the fifth item in Act 1 of this memorable review, which also included the song "Body and Soul." Libby Holman and Fred MacMurray are seen here. The "three" of the show title were Libby Holman, Clifton Webb and Fred Allen.

1930

100

FIVE-STAR FINAL, by Louis Weitzenkorn. Dec. 30, 1930. Cort Theatre. 175 perf. Prod.: A. H. Woods. Dir.: Worthington Miner. Sets: P. Dodd Ackerman. Act 2, Scene 6, the Townsend apartment (center) and two offices in the *Evening Gazette* building. Nancy Voorhees Townsend, whose unhappy past is being rehashed by the paper as a circulation-raising stunt, to the detriment of her daughter's marriage plans, phones to beg that the story be killed, but both the callous owner Hinchliffe and the remorseful managing editor Randall avoid speaking with her. Left to right on stage level: Hinchliffe's secretary, Miss Edwards (Madeleine Marshall); Hinchliffe (Berton Churchill); Mrs. Townsend (Merle Maddern, a cousin of Mrs. Fiske); Randall (Arthur Byron); and Randall's secretary, Miss Taylor (Helene Sinnott). In a tower above the furthest left of the three revolving stages sits the *Gazette* exchange operator (Lillian Bronson). Film technique obviously inspired the quick scene changes and "split-screen" effects. (Photo: White)

1931

101
GREEN GROW THE LILACS, by Lynn Riggs. Jan. 26, 1931. Guild Theatre. 64 perf. Prod.: The Theatre Guild. Dir.: Herbert J. Biberman. Sets: Raymond Sovey. Scene 2, the exterior of the Williams farmhouse in Indian Territory (Oklahoma), 1900, with the interior of Laurey Williams' bedroom. Laurey (June Walker), the itinerant Syrian peddler (Lee Strasberg), Ado Annie Carnes (Ruth Chorpenning) and Aunt Eller Murphy (Helen Westley) start violently as they hear a pistol shot from the direction of the smokehouse where the morose hired hand Jeeter Fry lives. This folk play featured many old songs and traditional ballads, and had 25 real cowboys in the cast. It was the basis for the musical *Oklahoma!* (Photo: Vandamm)

1931

102
THE BARRETTS OF WIMPOLE STREET, by Rudolf Besier. Feb. 9, 1931. Empire Theatre. 370 perf. Prod.: Katharine Cornell. Dir.: Guthrie McClintic. Set & costumes: Jo Mielziner. Elizabeth Barrett's bed-sitting room. Act 1, the bedridden Elizabeth (Katharine Cornell) is being entertained by her brothers and sisters when their overbearing father Edward Moulton-Barrett (Charles Waldron, far left) bursts in upon them. His oldest daughter, Arabel (Joyce Carey), is seated; the youngest, Henrietta (Margaret Barker), is standing. The room is furnished according to a description in one of Elizabeth Barrett's letters. This was Katharine Cornell's bow as a producer. The play was first performed at the 1930 Malvern Festival in England, then in London later that year (Sept. 23, Queen's Theatre). (Photo: Vandamm)

1931

103

THE WONDER BAR, by Géza Herczeg & Karl Farkas (adapted by Irving Caesar & Aben Kandel from *Die Wunder-Bar*); music by Robert Katscher. Mar. 17, 1931. Bayes Theatre. 76 perf. Prod.: Morris Gest, in association with the Messrs. Shubert, Dir.: William Mollison (dance direction by John Pierce). Set: Watson Barratt. Costumes: Charles LeMaire & others. A dance divertissement during the course of the action. The stage was extended by a large apron, holding tables, liquor bars, and the like, to simulate a Parisian cabaret. The rest of the theater was decorated in matching colors and designs. The plot was punctuated by songs, dances and specialties. Dramatic scenes were picked out in lights. This marked Al Jolson's return to Broadway after five years in Hollywood. Originally performed in Vienna, *The Wonder Bar* opened in London (Savoy Theatre), in a different English version, on Dec. 5, 1930. (Photo: White)

1931

104

THE BAND WAGON, by George S. Kaufman & Howard Dietz; music by Arthur Schwartz. June 3, 1931. New Amsterdam Theatre. 260 perf. Prod.: Max Gordon. Dir.: Hassard Short (dance direction by Albertina Rasch; all supervised by Dietz).

Sets: Albert Johnson. Costumes: Kiviette, Constance Ripley & others. This is the "White Heat" number (two numbers before the grand finale) from Act 2 of this highly prestigious revue. Adele and Fred Astaire are in the center.

105
THE HOUSE OF CONNELLY, by Paul Green. Sept. 28, 1931. Martin Beck Theatre. 91 perf. Prod.: The Group Theatre, Inc., under the auspices of The Theatre Guild. Dir.: Lee Strasberg & Cheryl Crawford. Sets: Cleon Throckmorton. Costumes: Fania Mindell. Act 1, Scene 2, the dining room of Connelly Hall on a decayed Southern plantation, about 1905. At Christmas supper, Robert Connelly (Morris Carnovsky), worthless brother of the late, great General Connelly, toasts the Gen- eral's widow Ellen (Mary Morris) on the 150th anniversary of the building of the house. Ellen's children are Evelyn (Eunice Stoddard), Will (Franchot Tone) and Geraldine (Stella Adler). This was the first major production of the Group Theatre, an offshoot of the Theatre Guild. They changed the playwright's original grim ending to one that implied the pos- sibility of social regeneration. (Photo: Vandamm)

106

THE CAT AND THE FIDDLE, by Jerome Kern & Otto Harbach; music by Kern. Oct. 15, 1931. Globe Theatre. Prod.: Max Gordon. Dir.: Jose Ruben (dance direction by Albertina Rasch). Sets: Henry Dreyfuss. Costumes: Constance Ripley & Kiviette. Act 1, Scene 1, a quay in Brussels. Pompineau, the music vendor (George Meader), sings "The Night Was Made for Love" to the Roumanian classical composer Victor Florescu (George Metaxa) and the American popular composer Shirley Sheridan (Bettina Hall), who have just met. Prominent in the foreground is the vegetable vendor, Mère Abajour (Lucette Valsy); far in the background is the book vendor (George Kirk). The Kern score also included "She Didn't Say 'Yes'" and "[I Watch] The Love Parade." (Photo: White)

1931

107
MOURNING BECOMES ELECTRA, by Eugene O'Neill. Oct. 26, 1931. Guild Theatre. 150 perf. Prod.: The Theatre Guild. Dir.: Philip Moeller. Sets & costumes: Robert Edmond Jones. Part 2 of the trilogy [*The Hunted*], Act 4, the stern of Adam Brant's clipper ship moored at a Boston wharf; for this scene, a section of the ship is removed to show the interior of the cabin. Orin Mannon (Earle Larimore), egged on by his sister Lavinia (Alice Brady), has just killed Captain Adam Brant (Thomas Chalmers), their mother's lover, for whose sake she murdered their father. This American version of the *Oresteia,* with the Trojan War replaced by the Civil War, and Argos by bleakest New England, was presented with a dinner intermission of one hour after Part 1. (Photo: Vandamm)

1931

108
OF THEE I SING, by George S. Kaufman & Morrie Ryskind; lyrics by Ira Gershwin; music by George Gershwin. Dec. 26, 1931. Music Box. 441 perf. Prod.: Sam H. Harris. Dir.: George S. Kaufman (dance & ensemble direction by Georgie Hale). Sets: Jo Mielziner. Costumes: Weld & others. Act 2, Scene 1, the President's office in the White House. The new President, John P. Wintergreen (William Gaxton), and his first lady, née Mary Turner (Lois Moran), attend to the nation's business with the aid of their respective secretaries, Sam Jenkins (George Murphy) and Miss Benson (June O'Dea). This was the first musical to receive a Pulitzer Prize (for 1931/32). The score included the title song, as well as "Who Cares" and "Love Is Sweeping the Country." (Photo: White)

1932

109

THE ANIMAL KINGDOM, by Philip Barry. Jan. 12, 1932. Broadhurst Theatre. 183 perf. Prod.: Gilbert Miller & Leslie Howard. Dir.: Gilbert Miller. Sets: Aline Bernstein. Dresses by Bergdorf Goodman. Act 3, Scene 1, the former library of Tom Collier's house, in the country near New York, now converted to a *comme-il-faut* dining room by his wife Cecelia. At breakfast on the morning after his hectic birthday party, the young publisher Tom Collier (Leslie Howard) is offered a glass of milk punch by his bluff and hearty butler Regan (William Gargan). Cecelia (Lora Baxter) is vexed by Regan's having been rehired. Also at the table are Tom's friend Owen Arthur (G. Albert Smith) and Cecelia's friend Grace Macomber (Ilka Chase). This was one of Barry's chief contributions to the theater of the 1930s. (Photo: Vandamm)

1933

110
DESIGN FOR LIVING, by Noel Coward. Jan. 24, 1933. Ethel Barrymore Theatre. 135 perf. Prod.: Max Gordon. Dir.: Noel Coward. Sets: Gladys E. Calthrop. Lynn Fontanne's gowns by Bergdorf Goodman. Act 3, Scene 1, the Friedmans' New York penthouse. Gilda Friedman (Lynn Fontanne) is unexpectedly visited by the two men in her past, the playwright Leo (Noel Coward) and the painter Otto (Alfred Lunt). In the actual production there would have been other actors on stage. Coward wrote the play with Lunt, Fontanne and himself specifically in mind. (Photo: Vandamm)

1933

111
ALIEN CORN, by Sidney Howard. Feb. 20, 1933. Belasco Theatre. 98 perf. Prod.: Katharine Cornell. Dir.: Guthrie McClintic. Set. Cleon Throckmorton. Katharine Cornell's dresses by Hélène Pons Studio. The living room of a small house on the campus of a women's college in the Middle West. Act 1: Elsa Brandt (Katharine Cornell), who hopes to be a concert pianist but must teach music to support herself and her father, is moving into a new house on the campus. Her father, Ottokar Brandt (Siegfried Rumann), embittered, irascible, homesick for Vienna, looks on. They are aided in their unpacking by Mrs. Skeats (Jessie Busley), a professor's wife, and by members of the faculty. Katharine Cornell's performance was more highly regarded than the play. (Photo: Vandamm)

1933

112

MEN IN WHITE, by Sidney Kingsley, Sept. 6, 1933. Broadhurst Theatre. 351 perf. Prod.: The Group Theatre, Inc. Sidney Harmon & James R. Ullman. Dir.: Lee Strasberg. Set: Mordecai Gorelik. Act 2, Scene 4, the operating room in St. George's Hospital: the minute preparations for an operation to save a nurse suffering from an abortion after an affair with one of the young doctors. This scene was done largely in pantomime. Painstaking didacticism characterized this production, which was Kingsley's first play, the Group Theatre's first financial success and the Pulitzer Prize winner for 1933/34. There was a unit set, with a permanent abstract background, and changes of locale within the hospital indicated by screens and props. (Photo: Vandamm)

1933

113
AH, WILDERNESS!, by Eugene O'Neill. Oct. 2, 1933. Guild Theatre. 289 perf. Prod.: The Theatre Guild. Dir.: Philip Moeller. Sets: Robert Edmond Jones. Act 2, Scene 1 [in the text, Act 3, Scene 1], the back room of a bar in a small hotel in a Connecticut town, 1906. Richard Miller (Elisha Cook, Jr.), who has come to the bar to learn about life, is stupefied with drink and afraid of the little prostitute Belle (Ruth Holden). The bartender (Donald McClelland) is annoyed by the racket that the traveling salesman (John Butler) has been making while ribbing the boy. The larger-than-life old-timer George M. Cohan was featured as Richard's father, but O'Neill was correct in pointing out that the boy is the main character of the play.

1933

114
MARY OF SCOTLAND, by Maxwell Anderson. Nov. 27, 1933. Alvin Theatre. 248 perf. Prod.: The Theatre Guild. Dir.: Theresa Helburn. Sets & costumes: Robert Edmond Jones. Act 3, a prison room in Carlisle Castle. Elizabeth Tudor (Helen Menken) has come to urge the abdication of her captive, Mary Stuart (Helen Hayes), but Mary is still triumphant, for she has known true love. This was one of Anderson's strongest verse dramas, and provided a fine role for Helen Hayes. (Photo: Vandamm)

1934

115

FOUR SAINTS IN THREE ACTS, words by Gertrude Stein; music by Virgil Thomson; scenario by Maurice Grosser. Feb. 20, 1934. 44th Street Theatre. 48 perf. Prod.: Harry Moses. Dir.: John Houseman (dance direction by Frederick Ashton). Sets & costumes: Florine Stettheimer & Kate Drain Lawson. Lighting: Abe Feder. A moment of the "action"— probably the Act 1 trio "They never knew about it green"— grouping (left to right) St. Teresa II (Bruce Howard), St. Ignatius (Edward Matthews) and St. Teresa I (Beatrice Robinson-Wayne). Part of the famous cellophane cyclorama and scenery is visible. The all-Black cast was Virgil Thomson's idea, which he had to defend staunchly. *Four Saints* had the longest continuous run of any American opera up to its time. Its first performance (which cannot really be considered a tryout) was at the Wadsworth Athenaeum, Hartford, on Feb. 7, 1934, sponsored by the Friends and Enemies of Modern Music. (Photo: White)

1934

116
THEY SHALL NOT DIE, by John Wexley. Feb. 20, 1934. Royale Theatre. 62 perf. Prod.: The Theatre Guild. Dir.: Philip Moeller. Sets: Lee Simonson. Act 3, Scene 2, a Southern courtroom. The brilliant New York defense attorney Nathan G. Rubin (Claude Rains) interrogates Lucy Wells (Ruth Gordon), who admits she was lying at an earlier trial when she stated she was raped by several Blacks; the Black defendant is Heywood Parsons (Al Stokes); behind Lucy is the Judge (Thurston Hall). This play was based closely on the 1931 Scottsboro case in Alabama. (Photo: Vandamm)

1934

117
YELLOW JACK, by Sidney Howard (in collaboration with Paul de Kruif). Mar. 6, 1934. Martin Beck Theatre. 79 perf. Prod. & dir.: Guthrie McClintic. Set: Jo Mielziner. Continuous-action play, moving uninterruptedly through changes of time and locale. At this point we are at Columbia Barracks at Quemado, near Havana, 1900. The American soldiers Levi P. Busch (Sam Levene, on stairs) and Warren G. McClelland (Edward Acuff) prepare to replace the shirtless John J. O'Hara (James Stewart) and Brinkerhof (Myron McCormick) in the special shack designed for a controlled experiment to prove that yellow fever is carried by mosquitoes. The central area of the top level of the unit set, reached by two staircases, represented throughout Walter Reed's lab; the lattice closed it off when not in use, or rolled around to form a background. Other equipment was pushed on from the sides at stage level. Changes of place were indicated by the lighting.

1934

118
STEVEDORE, by Paul Peters & George Sklar. Apr. 18, 1934. Civic Repertory Theatre. 111 perf. Prod.: The Theatre Union, Inc. Dir.: Michael Blankfort & Irving Gordon. Sets: Sointu Syrjala. Act 3, Scene 2, a courtyard in a Black neighborhood in New Orleans. Threatened with mob violence in the wake of a trumped-up rape charge and union agitation on the docks, the inhabitants raise a barricade and fight back. Binnie (Abbie Mitchell), holding the rifle, has shot the White ringleader. Ruby Oxley (Edna Thomas) bends over the body of the Black spokesman Lonnie Thompson (Jack Carter). Parts of the plot were based on several real incidents of labor disputes and attacks on Black workers dating back to 1919. The Theatre Union was a nonprofit membership organization producing plays of social content at low prices. (Photo: Vandamm)

1934

119

THE GREAT WALTZ, adapted by Moss Hart from the libretto by A. M. Willner, Heinz Reichert, Ernst Marischka, Caswell Garth & Desmond Carter; lyrics by Desmond Carter; music by Johann Strauss, father & son. Sept. 22, 1934. Center Theatre. 298 perf. Prod.: Max Gordon. Dir., lighting & effects: Hassard Short (dance direction by Albertina Rasch). Sets: Albert Johnson. Costumes: Doris Zinkeisen & Irene Sharaff. Act 2, Scene 5, Dommayer's ballroom in Vienna. The climax of the play: after many tribulations, Johann Strauss, Jr. (Guy Robertson), finally has the opportunity to conduct his music—especially "The Blue Danube"—in public. At the sides: the sympathetic Countess Olga Baranskaja (Marie Burke) and the hitherto unsympathetic Johann Strauss, Sr. (H. Reeves-Smith). In this scene, the pit orchestra rose to stage level and then moved upstage, leaving room for dancers. The elaborate production also included simulated fireworks. This was the first live show at the Center Theatre, which had been showing films since 1932. The original Viennese production was called *Walzer aus Wien*. The British version, further adapted for this American one, was called *Waltzes from Vienna* and opened at the London Alhambra on Aug. 17, 1931. (Photo: Vandamm)

1934

120
THE CHILDREN'S HOUR, by Lillian Hellman. Nov. 20, 1934. Maxine Elliott's Theatre. 691 perf. Prod. & dir.: Herman Shumlin. Sets: Aline Bernstein & Sointu Syrjala. Katherine Emmet's costumes by Henri Bendel, Inc. Children's costumes by De Pinna. Act 2, Scene 2, the living room of Mrs. Amelia Tilford's home. Dr. Joseph Cardin, fiancé of Karen Wright, who is co-director with Martha Dobie of a school for girls, interrogates the evil-minded child Mary Tilford, who has convinced her over-fond grandmother, Mrs. Tilford, that Karen and Martha are lovers. Left to right: Cardin (Robert Keith), Martha (Anne Revere), Mary (Florence McGee), Karen (Katherine Emery), Mrs. Tilford (Katherine Emmet). This was Lillian Hellman's vastly successful first play, based on an actual scandal case in nineteenth-century Scotland. (Photo: Vandamm)

121
GOLD EAGLE GUY, by Melvin Levy. Nov. 28, 1934. Morosco Theatre. 65 perf. Prod.: The Group Theatre, Inc., in association with D. A. Doran, Jr. Dir.: Lee Strasberg (dance direction by Helen Tamiris). Sets: Donald Oenslager. Costumes: Kay Morrison. Scene 2, the office of the Keane Shipping Company on a waterfront street in San Francisco, 1864. Adam Keane's fiancée, Jessie Sargent (Margaret Barker), is also desired by Keane's associate, the unscrupulous adventurer Guy Button. She is just leaving when she meets the banker who finances Button, Will Parrott (Morris Carnovsky), and Parrott's mistress, the actress Adah Menken (Stella Adler). Upper level, left to right: Button (J. Edward Bromberg), Keane (Walter Coy) and their clerk Ed Walker (Russell Collins). Adah Menken's life was lengthened in the play beyond the facts of history. The physical setting and lively direction were more memorable than the script. (Photo: Vandamm)

1935

122

THE OLD MAID, by Zoë Akins (from the novel by Edith Wharton). Jan. 7, 1935. Empire Theatre. 305 perf. Prod.: Harry Moses. Dir.: Guthrie McClintic. Sets & costumes: Stewart Chaney. Fourth episode [Act 3, Scene 1], the drawing room in the Ralston house on Gramercy Square, 1853. Tina, Charlotte Lovell's illegitimate daughter by the man whom she and her cousin Delia both loved, has been brought up by Delia—now the widow of James Ralston—without the knowledge of her true relationship to Charlotte, whom she resents. Left to right: Charlotte (Helen Menken); Delia's son-in-law, John Halsey (Warren Trent); Delia's daughter, Dee (Florence Williams); Delia (Judith Anderson); Tina (Margaret Anderson); and John's cousin, Lanning Halsey, Tina's fiancé (John Cromwell). This was Stewart Chaney's first New York assignment. The loudest outcries over the oft-disputed Pulitzer Prizes arose when this beautifully mounted and performed soap opera won the 1934/35 prize over the competition of *The Children's Hour, The Petrified Forest, Awake and Sing!* and *Valley Forge.* (Photo: Vandamm)

1935

123
AWAKE AND SING!, by Clifford Odets. Feb. 19, 1935. Belasco Theatre. 209 perf. Prod.: The Group Theatre, Inc. Dir.: Harold Clurman. Set: Boris Aronson. The Bergers' apartment on Longwood Avenue in the Bronx. Act 2, Scene 1: a panorama of the household. Left to right: Ralph Berger (Jules—later John—Garfield), disgruntled son of Myron and Bessie; disillusioned old Jacob (Morris Carnovsky), father of Morty and Bessie; Morty (J. Edward Bromberg), owner of a garment shop; Bessie Berger (Stella Adler), the lady of the house; Moe Axelrod (Luther Adler), wiseguy, friend of the family, in love with the daughter, Hennie; Sam Feinschreiber (Sanford Meisner), recent immigrant, who married Hennie Berger without knowing she was pregnant by another man; and Myron Berger (Art Smith), the man of the house. Feinschreiber was not actually on stage during the haircut. This was one of the major achievements of the Group Theatre. (Photo: Vandamm)

1935

124

WINTERSET, by Maxwell Anderson. Sept. 25, 1935. Martin Beck Theatre. 195 perf. Prod. & dir.: Guthrie McClintic. Sets: Jo Mielziner. Costumes: Eaves Costume Co. Act 1, Scene 3, a river bank under a bridgehead (intended as the Brooklyn end of the Brooklyn Bridge). Mio Romagna (Burgess Meredith), vengeful young son of an unjustly executed man, abuses the policeman (Anthony Blair) who has come to stop the playing of a street piano. Among the listeners are the apple woman Piny (Fernanda Eliscu); Judge Gaunt (Richard Bennett), who had presided at the case of Mio's father and is now maddened by remorse; a sailor (St. John Terrell); and—second from the right—Miriamne (Margo), sister of a man implicated in the crime. This play won the first New York Drama Critics Circle Award, 1935/36. Anderson's original conception of this set was a grim cityscape; it was Mielziner who suggested the view of the bridge span as an element of light and hope. (Photo: Vandamm)

125
JUBILEE, by Moss Hart; lyrics & music by Cole Porter. Oct. 12, 1935. Imperial Theatre. 169 perf. Prod.: Sam H. Harris & Max Gordon. Dir. & lighting: Hassard Short (dialogue direction by Monty Woolley; dance direction by Albertina Rasch). Sets: Jo Mielziner. Costumes: Irene Sharaff & Connie De Pinna. Act 2, Scene 7, the throne room of the palace. After a week of forbidden escapades, the royal family return to their official duties on the occasion of the King's jubilee. To the right of the Queen (Mary Boland) and King (Melville Cooper) are their children, Princess Diana (Margaret Adams) and Prince James (Charles Walters). In the aisle between courtiers and soldiers are the two little princes Rudolph (Jackie Kelk) and Peter (Montgomery Clift). Along the left foreground are those being honored for showing royalty an unwonted good time: Charles Rausmiller (Mark Plant), who plays the jungle hero Mowgli in films; the playwright and songwriter Eric Dare (Derek Williams); the party-giver Eva Standing (May Boley); and the American nightclub singer Karen O'Kane (June Knight). The rich and varied score included "Begin the Beguine" and "Just One of Those Things."

1935

126

DEAD END, by Sidney Kingsley. Oct. 28, 1935. Belasco Theatre. 687 perf. Prod. & set: Norman Bel Geddes. Dir.: Sidney Kingsley. The dead end of a street in the Fifties and an East River wharf; squalid tenements alongside the rear of an exclusive apartment house. End of Act 2: the public enemy Baby-Face Martin (Joseph Downing) who came back to his old neighborhood to visit his mother and old girl friend, has been killed by the G-man Bob, who has been wounded himself (Francis de Sales). At the right is Gimpty (Theodore Newton), who informed the police. Among the various "Dead End Kids" visible are Angel (Bobby Jordan), Dippy (Huntz Hall) and "TB" (Gabriel Dell). This, Kingsley's second play, had one of the most famous sets in theater history. (Photo: White)

1935

127
BOY MEETS GIRL, by Bella & Sam Spewack. Nov. 27, 1935.
Cort Theatre. 669 perf. Prod. & dir.: George Abbott. Sets:
Arne Lundborg. Dresses by Phil MacDonald. Act 2, Scene 3,
the office of C. Elliot Friday, a Hollywood producer. In order
to retain their control of an infant film star, the screen
writers Robert Law and J. Carlyle Benson have tricked the
young actor Rodney Bevan into publicly announcing that he
is the father, thus ruining the marriage plans of the child's
unwed mother, Susie. Left to right: Law (Allyn Joslyn), Benson (Jerome Cowan), Susie (Joyce Arling), Friday (Royal
Beal), Rodney (James MacColl) and a studio officer (George
W. Smith). The Spewacks had spent a lot of time writing
scenarios in Hollywood, and knew whereof they spoke in this
long-running hit. (Photo: Vandamm)

1935

128
VICTORIA REGINA, by Laurence Housman. Dec. 26, 1935. Broadhurst Theatre. 517 perf. Prod. & dir.: Gilbert Miller. Sets & costumes: Rex Whistler. Act 3, Scene 1, a garden tent at Balmoral Castle in 1877. Queen Victoria (Helen Hayes), who has now been reigning for forty years, awaits a visit from her Prime Minister, Disraeli. The play, a loosely knit selection of ten scenes from the Queen's life out of at least thirty written by Housman, was first performed at the Gate Theatre (a private-membership theater), London, on May 1, 1935. Censorship had to be lifted by Edward VIII before the first British public performance was possible, at the Lyric Theatre, London, on June 21, 1937, the hundredth anniversary of the Queen's coronation. The American production was one of Helen Hayes's greatest successes. (Photo: Vandamm)

1936

129
ETHAN FROME, by Owen & Donald Davis (from the novel by Edith Wharton, and suggested by a previous dramatization by Lowell Barrington). Jan. 21, 1936. National Theatre. 120 perf. Prod.: Max Gordon. Dir.: Guthrie McClintic. Sets & costumes: Jo Mielziner. Act 2, Scene 2, the kitchen of Ethan Frome's farmhouse in northern New England. Zenobia (Pauline Lord), Ethan's querulous, medicine-swilling wife, jealous of the attraction felt by Frome (Raymond Massey) for her sprightly cousin Mattie Silver (Ruth Gordon), who has come to live in the house and help out, leaves on a trip—ostensibly just to consult a new doctor, but really also to hire a girl to replace Mattie. Critics called this one of the very best adaptations of a work of fiction to the stage. (Photo: Vandamm)

1936

130
IDIOT'S DELIGHT, by Robert E. Sherwood. Mar. 24, 1936. Shubert Theatre. 300 perf. Prod.: The Theatre Guild. Dir.: Bretaigne Windust (supervised by Alfred Lunt & Lynn Fontanne; dance direction by Morgan Lewis); Set: Lee Simonson. Lynn Fontanne's clothes by Valentina. The cocktail lounge of the Hotel Monte Gabriele in the Italian Alps. Act 1: Donald Navadel (Barry Thompson), the hotel's social director, welcomes a new arrival, the glamorous "White Russian" Irene (Lynn Fontanne). Something about her seems familiar to the low-grade impresario Harry Van (Alfred Lunt), who has been herding a bunch of strip artists around Europe. Pulitzer Prize 1935/36. (Photo: Vandamm)

1936

131

WHITE HORSE INN, by Hans Müller & Erik Charell (from the play by Oskar Blumenthal & Gustav Kadelburg; adapted by David Freedman); lyrics by Irving Caesar; music by Ralph Benatzky & others. Oct 1, 1936. Center Theatre. 223 perf. Prod.: Laurence Rivers, Inc. Dir.: Erik Charell (dance direction by Max Rivers). Sets & costumes: Ernst Stern. Modern dresses: Irene Sharaff. Lighting: Eugene Braun. Act 2, Scene 10, the landing stage for lake steamers and the entire village on the Wolfgangssee in Austria. Confused by the solemnity of the occasion, and saddened by his hopeless love for the beautiful innkeeper, Leopold, headwaiter of the White Horse Inn (William Gaxton), stumbles badly in his welcoming speech to Emperor Franz Josef (Arnold Korff). Alfred Drake was in the male chorus of this production. The original German-language operetta, *Im Weissen Rössl,* was premiered in the Grosses Schauspielhaus, Berlin, on Nov. 8, 1930. A different English adaptation opened at the London Coliseum on Apr. 8, 1931. (Photo: Lucas-Pritchard)

1936

132
TOVARICH, by Jacques Deval (adapted by Robert E. Sherwood). Oct. 15, 1936. Plymouth Theatre. 356 perf. Prod. & dir.: Gilbert Miller. Sets: Raymond Sovey. Act 2, Scene 2, the kitchen of the wealthy Dupont home in Paris. Prince Mikail (John Halliday) and Grand Duchess Tatiana (Marta Abba), impoverished White Russians working as servants, are requested by the hated Soviet petroleum commissar Gorot-chenko (Cecil Humphreys) to hand over the fortune entrusted to them by the Tsar, since the money would save parts of Russian soil from falling into the hands of West European financiers. The distinguished Italian actress Marta Abba created several Pirandello roles. The original French production, *Tovaritch,* opened at the Théâtre de Paris, in Paris, on Oct. 13, 1933. (Photo: Vandamm)

1936

133
STAGE DOOR, by George S. Kaufman & Edna Ferber. Oct. 22, 1936. Music Box. 169 perf. Prod.: Sam H. Harris. Dir.: George S. Kaufman. Sets: Donald Oenslager. Costumes supervised by John Hambleton. Act 3, Scene 1, a Sunday morning in the main room of the Footlights Club, a dwelling for actresses in the West Fifties. Terry Randall (Margaret Sullavan, standing, center, with paper)—for whom the stage is a family religion, and film work a deed of darkness—is seen in the midst of her fellow lodgers, among whom are: (far left) Bernice Niemeyer (Janet Fox, a niece of Edna Ferber), (on couch, in riding clothes) Kendall Adams (Margot Stevenson), (at piano) Olga Brandt (Sylvia Lupas), (on piano) Pat Devine (Virginia Rousseau), (in armchair) Judith Canfield (Lee Patrick), (leaning on armchair) "Big Mary" Harper (Beatrice Blinn), (far right) "Little Mary" McCune (Mary Wickes). (Photo: Vandamm)

1936

134

YOU CAN'T TAKE IT WITH YOU, by Moss Hart & George S. Kaufman. Dec. 14, 1936. Music Box. 837 perf. Prod.: Sam H. Harris. Dir.: George S. Kaufman. Set: Donald Oenslager. Costumes supervised by John Hambleton. The "every-man-for-himself" room in the home of Martin Vanderhof and the Sycamores, near Columbia University. End of Act 2: the Kirbys, wealthy parents of Alice Sycamore's fiancé, have come for a visit on the wrong night and are stunned by the normal pandemonium of the household. Left to right: a G-man; Mr. De Pinna, a house guest for years (Frank Conlan); Paul Sycamore, Alice's father (Frank Wilcox); his wife Penelope (Josephine Hull); their other daughter Essie (Paula Trueman); her husband, Ed Carmichael (George Heller); Martin Vanderhof, Penelope's father (Henry Travers); Boris Kolenkhov, Essie's dancing teacher (George Tobias); Alice (Margot Stevenson); Donald, the housemaid's friend (Oscar Polk); two G-men; the drunken actress Gay Wellington (Mitzi Hajos); Anthony Kirby, Jr. (Jess Barker); his mother, Miriam Kirby (Virginia Hammond); his father (William J. Kelly). Pulitzer Prize 1936/37. (Photo: Vandamm)

1936

135

BROTHER RAT, by John Monks, Jr., & Fred F. Finklehoffe. Dec. 16, 1936. Biltmore Theatre. 577 perf. Prod. & dir.: George Abbott. Sets: Cirker & Robbins. Cadet uniforms from various sources, including Alumni of Virginia Military Institute. Act 3, Scene 1, outside the barracks of the Virginia Military Institute, Lexington, Va. Three delinquent cadets walking penalty tours are visited by the girl friends of two of them. Left to right: Billy Randolph (Frank Albertson); his girl, Joyce Winfree (Wyn Cahoon); the secretly married cadet Bing Edwards (Eddie Albert); Claire Ramm, the Colonel's daughter (Mary Mason); her beau, Dan Crawford (Jose Ferrer). "Brother rat" was a friendly greeting among VMI cadets. The authors were once cadets there, and had madcap adventures similar to those in the play. (Photo: Lucas-Pritchard)

136
HIGH TOR, by Maxwell Anderson. Jan. 9, 1937. Martin Beck Theatre. 171 perf. Prod. & dir.: Guthrie McClintic. Sets: Jo Mielziner. Men's costumes by Hélène Pons Studio. Act 3, an elevated section of High Tor, a mountain on the Hudson River. The evil land grabber Art J. Biggs (Harold Moffet) and the venal Judge Skimmerhorn (Thomas W. Ross) have remained all night in the steam shovel where they were hoisted and left hanging by phantom Dutchmen. Their crooked schemes now come to light. Left to right at ground level: A. B. Skimmerhorn, the Judge's uncle (John M. Kline); John, a dying Indian (Harry Irvine); the owner of the land, Van Dorn (Burgess Meredith); a State trooper; the bank robbers Elkus (Hume Cronyn) and Dope (Leslie Gorall); a State trooper. New York Drama Critics Circle Award 1936/37. (Photo: Vandamm)

1937

137

(KING) RICHARD II, by William Shakespeare. Feb. 5, 1937. St. James Theatre. 133 perf. Prod.: Eddie Dowling & Robinson Smith. Dir.: Margaret Webster & Charles Alan. Sets & costumes: David Ffolkes. Act 1, Scene 1, King Richard's palace (Windsor Castle), 1398. Thomas Mowbray, Duke of Norfolk (William Post, Jr.), appears before the King (Maurice Evans) to accuse Henry Bolingbroke, Duke of Hereford, of treason. Bolingbroke (Ian Keith) is standing at the left. The hatless old man near the King is John of Gaunt (Augustin Duncan), Duke of Lancaster, uncle of the King and father of Bolingbroke. The elderly actor and director Augustin Duncan was virtually blind by this time, and could appear only in such roles as John of Gaunt. This was one of the most highly lauded Shakespearean productions of the century. The revival of the play in 1937 (after a 59-year lapse in America) was spurred by the abdication of Edward VIII. *King Richard II* was probably first performed at the Globe Theatre, London, on Feb. 7, 1601. (Photo: Vandamm)

1937

138
YES, MY DARLING DAUGHTER, by Mark Reed. Feb. 9, 1937. Playhouse. 405 perf. Prod. & dir.: Alfred de Liagre, Jr. Sets: Raymond Sovey. Costumes supervised by Adele Carples. Act 2, the upstairs room known as "Mother's Office" in the Murrays' summer home in New Canaan, Conn. The writer Ann Murray (Lucile Watson) entertains her daughter Ellen's young man, Douglas Hall (Boyd Crawford), while wondering whether to stop him from spending a weekend alone with the girl. Also present are the literary agent Titus Jaywood (Nicholas Joy), once Ann's lover in far-off Greenwich Village days, and Ellen (Peggy Conklin). Mark Reed had had plays produced on Broadway since 1919, but this charming comedy was his first real triumph. (Photo: Lucas-Pritchard)

1938

139

THE SHOEMAKERS' HOLIDAY, by Thomas Dekker (based on stories in Thomas Deloney's *Gentle Craft,* 1598). Jan. 1, 1938. Mercury Theatre. 69 perf. Prod.: Orson Welles & John Houseman. Dir. & set: Orson Welles. Costumes: Millia Davenport. Scene 16 [of full text], a street near St. Faith's Church, London, mid-fifteenth century. The merchant Master Hammon, who has tricked Jane into believing that her husband Ralph (or Rafe) Davenport was killed in the French wars, is now about to marry her, but reckons without Ralph, who has discovered the deception, and Ralph's fellow journeyman shoemakers Hodge (or Roger) and Firk. Left to right: Hammon (Vincent Price), Jane (Ruth Ford), two pages (Frederick Ross & John Berry), a serving man (William Allard), Hodge (Norman Lloyd), Ralph (Elliot Read), a boy (Arthur Anderson) and Firk (Hiram Sherman). The Mercury production began on the anniversary of the world premiere—at the English Court, on Jan. 1, 1600. The set included a burlap cyclorama and three framed inner stages, side by side. The intermissionless performance of the heavily cut text lasted just a little over an hour. (Photo: Lucas-Pritchard)

1938

140
OUR TOWN, by Thornton Wilder. Feb. 4, 1938. Henry Miller's Theatre. 336 perf. Prod. & dir.: Jed Harris (technical direction by Raymond Sovey). Almost no scenery. Costumes: Hélène Pons. Grover's Corners, N.H. End of Act 2, the year 1904: after their wedding ceremony, Emily Webb (Martha Scott) and George Gibbs (John Craven, son of Frank Craven) are descending from the stage and are about to run off through the auditorium. The Stage Manager (Frank Craven), who narrates and performs various little roles—he has just been the clergyman—stands beaming at them. This was the classic play of hometown contentment and the need to treasure the most minor moments of existence. Pulitzer Prize 1937/38. (Photo: Vandamm)

1938

141
ABE LINCOLN IN ILLINOIS, by Robert E. Sherwood. Oct. 15, 1938. Plymouth Theatre. 472 perf. Prod.: The Playwrights' Company (Maxwell Anderson, S. N. Behrman, Sidney Howard, Elmer Rice & Robert E. Sherwood). Dir.: Elmer Rice. Sets: Jo Mielziner. Act 3, Scene 4 [Scene 12 of play], the Springfield railroad station on Feb. 11, 1861. Lincoln (Raymond Massey), with his wife Mary (Muriel Kirkland) and their son Tad (Lloyd Barry) beside him, addresses friends and constituents before leaving for his inauguration in Washington. Pulitzer Prize 1938/39. (Photo: Vandamm)

1938

142
KNICKERBOCKER HOLIDAY, by Maxwell Anderson; music by Kurt Weill. Oct. 19, 1938. Ethel Barrymore Theatre. 168 perf. Prod.: The Playwrights' Company. Dir.: Joshua Logan (dance direction by Carl Randall & Edwin Denby). Sets: Jo Mielziner. Costumes: Frank Bevan. Act 2, Scene 2, the Battery as seen from the waterfront one night in 1647. The new governor, Pieter Stuyvesant (Walter Huston), dances with the maidens of New Amsterdam in the "Scars" number during his betrothal ceremony. To the right of him is the bride, Tina Tienhoven (Jeanne Madden). Robert Rounseville was in the male chorus of this production. (Photo: Lucas-Pritchard)

1938

143
THE BOYS FROM SYRACUSE, by George Abbott; lyrics by Lorenz Hart; music by Richard Rodgers (based on Shakespeare's *Comedy of Errors*). Nov. 23, 1938. Alvin Theatre. 235 perf. Prod. & dir.: George Abbott (dance direction by George Balanchine). Sets: Jo Mielziner. Costumes: Irene Sharaff. Act 1, Scene 5, the street outside the house of Antipholus of Ephesus. This is the act finale, "Let Antipholus In." He is debarred from entrance by his wife, who is unknowingly entertaining his long-lost twin brother, Antipholus of Syracuse. The house moved in and out as the action required. The score included "Falling in Love with Love" and "This Can't Be Love." (Photo: Vandamm)

1939

144

THE LITTLE FOXES, by Lillian Hellman. Feb. 15, 1939. National Theatre. 410 perf. Prod. & dir.: Herman Shumlin. Set: Howard Bay. Costumes: Aline Bernstein. The living room of the Giddens' house in a small Southern town, 1900. Act 2: Regina Hubbard Giddens and her brothers try to persuade her husband Horace, who is dying of heart disease, to put up his share of the money needed to build a cotton mill. Left to right: Regina (Tallulah Bankhead), Horace (Frank Conroy), Oscar Hubbard's son Leo (Dan Duryea), Ben Hubbard (Charles Dingle), Oscar Hubbard (Carl Benton Reid). *The Little Foxes* gave Tallulah Bankhead the most famous role of her career. The set designer, Howard Bay, had already made his mark in the Federal Theatre Project. (Photo: Vandamm)

1939

145
THE PHILADELPHIA STORY, by Philip Barry. Mar. 28, 1939. Shubert Theatre. 417 perf. Prod.: The Theatre Guild. Dir.: Robert B. Sinclair (supervised by Theresa Helburn & Lawrence Langner). Sets & lighting: Robert Edmond Jones. Act 1, the sitting room of the Lords's house in the country near Philadelphia. All the members of the family are startled to hear Tracy Lord address her Uncle Willie as "Papá"; she does not want the visiting magazine reporter and photographer to know that her reprobate father has not been invited to her impending second wedding. Left to right: Uncle Willie Tracy (Forrest Orr); the reporter, Macaulay ("Mike") Connor (Van Heflin); the photographer, Elizabeth ("Liz") Imbrie (Shirley Booth); Tracy's mother, Margaret Lord (Vera Allen); Tracy Lord (Katharine Hepburn); C. K. Dexter Haven (Joseph Cotten), Tracy's first husband, mischievously invited by Tracy's little sister Dinah; George Kittredge (Frank Fenton), the new fiancé; Dinah (Lenore Lonergan); and Tracy's brother Sandy (Dan Tobin). In the actual play, Dexter Haven does not enter for another few minutes. Written for Katharine Hepburn, then on the outs with Hollywood, this Barry comedy saved the Guild financially in one of its darkest hours. (Photo: Vandamm)

1939

146

THE MAN WHO CAME TO DINNER, by Moss Hart & George S. Kaufman. Oct. 16, 1939. Music Box. 739 perf. Prod.: Sam H. Harris. Dir.: George S. Kaufman. Set: Donald Oenslager. The home of Mr. and Mrs. Stanley in Mesalia, Ohio, 1938. End of Act 2: Sheridan Whiteside broadcasts an unctuous Christmas message from the home he has turned topsy-turvy since his confinement there with a broken hip. Left to right: the nurse, Miss Preen (Mary Wickes), who has just been bitten by a gift penguin; Dr. Bradley (Dudley Clements); the servants Sarah (Mrs. Priestly Morrison) and John (George Probert); Whiteside (Monty Woolley); the announcer, Westcott (Edward Fisher); two radio technicians (Rodney Stewart & Carl Johnson); six choir boys (Daniel Leone, Jack Whitman, Daniel Landon, Donald Landon, DeWitt Purdue & Robert Rea); the owners of the house, Ernest W. Stanley (George Lessey) and his wife (Virginia Hammond), who have just learned that their children have run away; the actress Lorraine Sheldon (Carol Goodner); and the local newspaperman Bert Jefferson (Theodore Newton). Whiteside was modeled on the critic and author Alexander Woollcott. (Photo: Vandamm)

1939

147
KEY LARGO, by Maxwell Anderson. Nov. 27, 1939. Ethel Barrymore Theatre. 105 perf. Prod.: The Playwrights' Company. Dir.: Guthrie McClintic. Sets: Jo Mielziner. Costumes: Hélène Pons. Act 1, a wharf on Key Largo. King McCloud (Paul Muni), a veteran of the Spanish Civil War who has come to visit the family of a dead comrade, finds their little hotel commandeered by tough gamblers who bilk passing tourists. At the roulette wheel is Murillo (Frederic Tozere); at the door, Hunk (Karl Malden). (Photo: Vandamm)

1939

148
DU BARRY WAS A LADY, by B. G. DeSylva & Herbert Fields; lyrics & music by Cole Porter. Dec. 6, 1939. 46th Street Theatre. 408 perf. Prod.: B. G. DeSylva. Dir.: Edgar McGregor (dance direction by Robert Alton). Sets & costumes: Raoul Pene Du Bois. Act 1, Louis Blore (Bert Lahr), who has just won the Irish sweepstakes, returns to his old stamping ground, the Club Petite, where he used to be a lavatory attendant. Part of the action occurred, as a dream sequence, at the court of Louis XV (also played by Bert Lahr), The score included "Katie Went to Haiti," sung by Ethel Merman, and "Friendship," a duet for the stars. (Photo: Lucas & Monroe)